"Perhaps Fleming Rutledge's greatest contribution to the moribund mainline church is her unflagging, exhilarating insistence that the entire structure of Christianity stands or falls on the foundation of three little words, 'And God said ...' Fleming trusts deeply in the power of the word to have its way with preachers, hearers, and readers alike. For that reason, I can think of no better friend than Fleming to follow into the strange, new world of the Bible where we are met by a living, loquacious God determined to be in conversation with us— *even* us. Fleming's work has long equipped me to climb into the pulpit every Sunday and dare to preach. Now, in the gift of this new devotional collection, arranged according to the liturgical year, her unyielding engagement with Scripture and her pastoral concern for the human situation will prove for readers what Fleming has been for me, a means of grace."

— JASON MICHELI
pastor, author, podcaster, and blogger at *Tamed Cynic*

"Fleming Rutledge is an astonishingly good preacher. Rooted in her conviction that the Bible is 'the authentic breathing voice of the Word of God,' she consistently draws out profound insights, new challenges, and joyful surprises from familiar and unfamiliar texts. Her sermons invite her hearers to expect God to speak specifically to them—to gain eyes to see how God is already creatively at work in their lives, and then gain courage to participate with God in that work. Laura Bardolph Hubers has given the world a beautiful gift with this devotional edition that will introduce many to Fleming Rutledge's sermons, and, in turn, to the living, merciful Word of God that they proclaim."

— CALEB MASKELL
Society of Vineyard Scholars

"I'm tempted to say two realities govern all of Fleming Rutledge's work— God and his gospel. But we might say it's just one—the grace of God at work in our salvation. Yet this is no cheap grace, no easy feat, no quiet spirituality for those who can muster the energy for self-improvement and self-actualization, but the grace of our Lord Jesus Christ who by the will of the Father in the power of the Spirit snatches hopeless sinners out of the jaws of sin, death, and the devil in the agony, judgment, and triumph of his cross and resurrection. And it is precisely this disruptive grace that we are blessed to reckon with on every page of this set of eloquent and energetic devotions. Laura Bardolph Hubers has done first-rate work in gathering and editing this collection of Rutledge's work for us."

— DEREK RISHMAWY
blogger at *Reformedish*

"This brilliant collection from Rutledge's sermons leads us into the beauty of the church calendar, in which time itself forms us in the truth of the gospel. That the themes of Rutledge's sermons naturally lend themselves to the pattern of the liturgical year is a testimony to the depth and range of her theological insight and her profound care for the church. Rutledge is not only a gifted theologian and homilist, but a profoundly gifted wordsmith as well, and her luminous prose gives insight on each page. I will be using this book for my own devotions, and I commend Rutledge's wisdom to the whole church."

— TISH HARRISON WARREN
author of *Liturgy of the Ordinary* and *Prayer in the Night*

"I cannot think of a more reliable guide to escort us through the church calendar with weekly devotions than Fleming Rutledge. Her love of holy Scripture and the sacred calendar combined with her half century of preaching expertise make *Means of Grace* a precious gift. From Advent through Ordinary Time, the words of Fleming Rutledge are indeed a means of grace to help us behold the glory of Christ."

— BRIAN ZAHND
author of *Sinners in the Hands of a Loving God*

"*Means of Grace* is exquisite. Fleming Rutledge's offerings here, curated and edited by Laura Bardolph Hubers, plumb the depth of human experience and electrify the Christian imagination. They re-enchant us, turn our gaze toward God, and anchor us in the good, the true, and the beautiful. Through them, grace reorients us. Rutledge is among the best preachers and teachers of our time—a wise soul. I can think of few others who can expertly guide us through the liturgical Christian year in such a robust and nurturing fashion. I need faithful and trustworthy leaders of depth, wise ones to look up to; Fleming Rutledge is such a person. Contemplate the words within these pages for your own good—and the good of others."

— MARLENA GRAVES
author of *The Way Up Is Down: Becoming Yourself by Forgetting Yourself*

"Fleming Rutledge picks you up, dusts you down, gives you a good talking to—but in such a way that leaves you more alive, more excited to be a Christian, more thrilled with God. Her fearless writing communicates to the reader that if you leave the kid gloves aside, you'll meet the real God—not the one lazy or complacent sermons have shown you before. *Tolle lege* as Augustine did—pick up and read—and you'll be invigorated by these injections of grace."

— SAMUEL WELLS
vicar of St. Martin-in-the-Fields, London

MEANS OF GRACE

A Year of Weekly Devotions

FLEMING RUTLEDGE

Edited by Laura Bardolph Hubers

WILLIAM B. EERDMANS PUBLISHING COMPANY

GRAND RAPIDS, MICHIGAN

Wm. B. Eerdmans Publishing Co.
4035 Park East Court SE, Grand Rapids, Michigan 49546
www.eerdmans.com

27 26 25 24 23 22 21   1 2 3 4 5 6 7

ISBN 978-0-8028-7870-0

Library of Congress Cataloging-in-Publication Data

Names: Rutledge, Fleming, author. | Hubers, Laura Bardolph,
    1988– editor.
Title: Means of grace : a year of weekly devotions / Fleming Rutledge ;
    edited by Laura Bardolph Hubers.
Description: Grand Rapids, Michigan : Wm. B. Eerdmans Publishing
    Company, [2021] | Includes bibliographical references. | Summary:
    "A weekly devotional culled from the sermons of Fleming Rut-
    ledge designed to be used within the framework of the liturgical
    calendar"—Provided by publisher.
Identifiers: LCCN 2021000658 | ISBN 9780802878700 (hardcover)
Subjects: LCSH: Church year—Prayers and devotions. | Episcopal
    Church—Sermons.
Classification: LCC BV30 .R88 2021 | DDC 242/.3—dc23
LC record available at https://lccn.loc.gov/2021000658

CONTENTS

EPIPHANY

LENT AND HOLY WEEK

EASTER

SEASON AFTER PENTECOST

EDITOR'S PREFACE

The task was simple but daunting: I had volunteered to write a review of Fleming Rutledge's *The Crucifixion* for the Eerdmans company blog, *Eerdword*. I was too new at my job in the Eerdmans marketing department to grasp the full measure of what I was taking on, but reading the manuscript had enthralled me. So I rushed in where angels fear to tread, nervous but determined to do my best with the assignment. I wrote in my brief blog post about the magnificence of Fleming's prose; the beautifully crafted sentences in the introduction alone gave me chills. It was clear that she delights in writing, and it spoke to my English-major heart.

I needn't have worried about the blog post going up. Fleming responded with the graciousness I have since come to know as one of her hallmarks. "I am so very grateful to you for responding to what I am trying to do, better than almost anyone," she wrote in an email to me. This was the beginning of one of the most important friendships of my life.

After that introduction to Fleming's writing, I started working backward, reading all the many sermons we'd published with her through the years. Over and over again I was struck by her unique gift for placing God's majesty and power and mercy in direct conversation with a real, empathetic understanding of human experience—all in a way that makes it clear she cherishes the power and beauty of language. Someone asked me once how I would summarize her preaching. I answered this way: God is God and we are not; he does not always act in the way we expect. He went so far in defying expectations of divinity as to enter the darkness of human suffering. So whatever doubts or hard questions you have about God, whatever pain you bring, the gospel can take it. There's a reason Fleming's first book was called The Bible and the "New York Times." Her preaching never strays from real life.

I have not been shy about sharing how much Fleming's work has shaped my understanding of the gospel. But I found pretty quickly that too many of my friends who (like me) had not been to seminary had never heard of her, much less sat down to read a book of her sermons. I was—I still am—convinced that her insights are for the whole church. I wanted to come up with a way of presenting those insights to a wider audience.

As I thought and read further, I realized that the answer lay in the turn toward the personal that Fleming always makes in her sermons. Her preaching is anything but abstract; she makes it clear that God is intimately tied to our everyday lives. With careful editing, the sermons would make ideal devotional material that anyone could feel prepared to pick up.

The sixty entries collected here are all taken from The Bible and the "New York Times," Help My Unbelief, The Undoing of Death, Not Ashamed of the Gospel, And God Spoke to Abraham, and Advent. I've removed some dated references—the product of Fleming's close attention to the news—and cut as necessary to make them uniform in length, but the heart of the message has been preserved in each case. I have imagined these being read weekly, with additional entries for particular days in the church calendar—Epiphany, Maundy Thursday, Good Friday, Pentecost, and Christmas Eve—but I hope readers will feel free to dip in and out. Each entry stands on its own. Fleming's work is so rich with insight that readers may even want to consider reading each entry more than once throughout the week.

In Fleming's preaching and Episcopal tradition, the liturgical calendar has played an important role. This book follows that calendar, and readers who wish to may join her in observing it by reading these devotions in keeping with that schedule. For those unfamiliar with the liturgical calendar and Revised Common Lectionary, the Vanderbilt Divinity School Library has a very helpful online resource.

A book of devotions requires prayers, of course. At the end of each entry you'll find a collect from one of Fleming's favorite repositories of prayer and language: the 1928 Book of Common Prayer. Since they are collects, they use the plural "we" instead of the personal "I." I have not changed that. I hope that readers will find that praying the collect helps them turn from inward reflection back outward, joining with the saints of God to do God's work in the world.

In preparing this volume, I spent eighteen months completely immersed in Fleming's work. I can only hope that through the work of the Holy Spirit readers will gain as much from reading it as I did from preparing it. I also hope it will spur them to pick up Fleming's previously published works, which are so beautifully crafted that I agonized over altering them in any way.

Fleming's presence in my life—in both her work and her friendship—has been one of my greatest gifts. It became clear early in our interactions, reinforced by regular in-person visits at conferences and in her home, that she is a kindred spirit. I am unspeakably grateful for her trust in me to allow me to compile this volume, and I do not take that privilege lightly.

The world is starved for truth and beauty. Read her words, and, by the power of the Holy Spirit, you will find both.

Laura Bardolph Hubers

Eighteen months ago, Laura Bardolph Hubers, the director of marketing and publicity at Eerdmans, approached me with a proposal to assemble and edit a book of my sermons for devotional purposes, ordered according to the church calendar. This was an astonishing gift. Readers may perhaps imagine how humbling it is, and how heart filling, to know that one's work is valued that much, especially by a person of Laura's qualities. I had come to know and appreciate Laura through the connection to Eerdmans—the publisher of all ten of my books—but this totally unexpected offering could only have been by the agency of the Holy Spirit, for it came without any hint or suggestion, let alone action, on my part.

I wish to emphasize that Laura put this together herself without any input from me whatsoever. I did not even look at the galleys or page proofs; I trust her that much. Furthermore, she has managed to do this while working full time at Eerdmans, maintaining a marriage and household, and raising two small children—an extraordinary feat.

Laura's efforts have been enthusiastically supported by David Bratt, executive editor at Eerdmans, who placed the resources of Eerdmans and his advocacy at Laura's disposal. My husband, Dick, and I have had the great pleasure of two visits from Laura and David in our home to discuss this project and others to come. These times of companionship have been a joy to us both, and it was a wonder to behold their commitment to sorting out my enormous collection of papers. I have so much confidence in Laura now, that I have asked her to be in charge of the disposition of my papers after my death, and she has agreed. This is of inestimable comfort to me. I thank God for the gracious gift of collaborating in such a generous project with two *simpatico* colleagues.

SINCE THIS MAY BE THE LAST collection of my sermons to be published in my lifetime, it seems to me that I should try to say something about preaching. I have done a good deal of teaching other preachers in an informal way in various settings, but only once have I taught it officially in an academic setting. That was in 2008 when I spent a full term at Wycliffe College in Toronto. I had thirty students in two courses. This was an opportunity to gather my thoughts about preaching into coherent form. I always intended to put all this together in a book about preaching. That now seems unlikely—though one never knows what the Spirit might do—so I will say a few things here about the fundamental theological convictions that have undergirded my forty-eight years of preaching, including the words collected here.

When I was at Wycliffe in the University of Toronto, I habitually walked through Victoria College, where there is a sculpture of the great literary critic Northrop Frye sitting on a bench. More than once I sat down beside him to express my thanks for his book *The Great Code*, in which he wrote, "The style of the Bible is of the battlefield rather than the cloister."[1] Similarly (and famously), Annie Dillard wrote that

> On the whole I do not find Christians, outside of the catacombs, sufficiently sensible of conditions. Does anyone have the foggiest idea what sort of power we so blithely invoke? It is madness to wear ladies' straw hats and velvet hats to church; we should all be wearing crash helmets.[2]

Too much of this, to be sure, would result in a perpetually heightened style of preaching, in which the preacher might come across as harsh and angry. The alternative, however, is all too common: sermons that seek simply to please and, perhaps, to persuade. Persuasion is not the best mode for preaching. There is very little persuading in Scripture. The sermon, when it is working, is neither a collection of spiritual reflections nor a program for sociopolitical action, but most essentially an event of the irresistible Word of God. When the Spirit is acting through both preacher and hearers, the living God creates something *ex opere operato*, as it were—"by the work worked," as in the classic formulation concerning the sacraments—only it is *by the Word worked*. The preacher is handling dynamite; her role is to prepare it and then get out of the way. (If the way lies in the direction of sociopolitical action, so much the better.)

My revered homiletics professor, Edmund Steimle, insisted that the preacher should always *illustrate*, never exhort. The Bible does not argue in favor of its positions. The Bible *shows* God powerfully at work and calls people to *participate* in what God is already doing. Preaching, therefore, is least itself when the listeners are feeling pressured to do something or be something. One of my sharpest memories in this regard is from the late 1960s, just before I started thinking of applying to seminary. I was teaching adult Sunday Bible classes on the Hebrew prophets. The senior warden of my church said to me after class, "Fleming, you're way out ahead of us." It was not a compliment. I did not understand why this was important till I'd had two years of seminary. I never took but one course in homiletics, but in just that one course Dr. Steimle took hold of a "public speaker" and would-be "prophetic" Bible teacher and made her into a biblical storyteller.

I was prepared to receive Steimle's teaching because I was taking courses in both systematic theology and Bible in my first year. I was learning Scripture and doctrine, not *seriatum*, but concurrently. That was the practice at Union Theological

Seminary at that time (1972). The idea was that the work of understanding doctrine was not done *subsequently to* studying Scripture but *concurrently with it*—demonstrating that there is an organic relationship at work. Theology and Scripture are continually in dialogue with one another.

The hoary notion that expository sermons should end with "application" should be retired. Illustrations, yes; applications, no. The Scripture does not teach precepts and principles that can be "applied"; in the Bible, we encounter not "life lessons" or "timeless teaching" but the living God present and acting in the story of redemption. Dorothy L. Sayers puts it unforgettably in her pungent style:

> It is the *dogma* that is the *drama*—not beautiful phrases, nor comforting sentiments, nor vague aspirations to loving-kindness and uplift, nor the promise of something nice after death—but the terrifying assertion that the same God Who made the world lived in the world and passed through the grave and gate of death.[3]

The sermon, then, is essentially a drama—a plot full of suspense, threat, failure, and emergency that culminates in God's own last-ditch rescue bid. The eighteenth-century English poet Christopher Smart captures some of this:

> Glorious, most glorious is the crown
> of him that brought salvation down
> by meekness, Mary's son.
> Seers that stupendous truth believed,
> and now the matchless deed's achieved,
> determined, dared, and done.[4]

Preaching the "matchless deed" of Jesus Christ requires daring. The preacher should be willing to take risks—not in the sense of taking unpopular stands, but the risk of proclaiming the radical gospel of God, who is "no respecter of persons" (Acts 10:34).[5] If the preacher is delivering sermons week in and week out, year by year, a correspondence to the events of the day both personal and corporate will grow organically out of the preaching—and if it doesn't, it must be said, the preacher is using some kind of filter to keep radical notions at bay. That will eventually result in blandness, and the gospel can never be bland. Sooner or later, if it is really the gospel, someone will say, as Ahab did to Elijah, "Is that you, O troubler of Israel?" (1 Kings 18:17). If Israel is never troubled by the preaching of the gospel, then it is not the gospel. Sooner or later the gospel will call for "good trouble, necessary trouble," as civil rights hero John Lewis was fond of saying, but it will be because it arises organically out of the message, not because the preacher is way out ahead of the congregation in self-righteousness. It took a long time for me to figure that out.

The one thing needful for preaching is a faithful commitment to the Bible as the authentic, breathing voice of the Word of God. A brief passage from Paul's first letter to the Thessalonian church should strengthen the preacher's conviction. The apostle is expressing affection and gratitude for this particularly beloved congregation. Notice what he says about the congregation of listeners:

> We know, brothers and sisters beloved by God, that he has chosen you; for our gospel came to you not only in word, but also in power and in the Holy Spirit and with full conviction.... And we also thank God constantly for this, that when you received the word of God which you heard from us [apostles], you accepted it not as the word of human beings but as what it really is, the word of God, which is at work in you believers. (1 Thess. 1:4–5; 2:13)

Black Christians still speak habitually of "the word" in just this way. Just a few days ago I heard an interview with a black

woman on the radio in which she referred to her recent Sunday worship, saying that "the minister brought us the Word."
This is a time-honored way of speaking among black churchgoers, and it carries with it an unselfconscious, foundational
presupposition: the Lord's living Word is spoken each week
through the messenger and is eagerly expected by the congregation. I had the joy of preaching in a congregation like
that at Grace Church in New York for fourteen years. In such
a situation, preaching is reciprocal. You can feel Paul's joy as
he writes to the Thessalonian Christians about their eager re-
ception of the Word. Part of the preacher's calling is to show
the congregation, week by week in the preaching, that God's
Word is indeed living and active, sharper than any two-edged
sword, able to judge the thoughts and intentions of the heart
(Heb. 4:12). I have often quoted Johnny Ray Youngblood, the
respected longtime pastor of a large African American church
in Brooklyn, where he was known for initiating a whole host of
social programs. Yet he said, "There's no substitute for preaching. I don't care what else a preacher does in the community or
what causes he promotes, the people want to know on Sunday
morning whether there's a word from the Lord." I believe that
every preacher should take this to heart and set about building
up a community of expectation.

This speaks directly to those who will be drawing on the sermons in this devotional book. Whether I have succeeded from
time to time in bringing a word from the Lord depends not only
on the preacher but also on the hearers—the "community of
expectation." Such a community can come into being *ex nihilo*,
so to speak, when the preaching arises out of the Word week
by week. A congregation can be trained, over time, to be ex-
pectant, awaiting "a word from the Lord." Sermons read on the
page do not have the unrepeatable immediacy of live preaching, but even at second hand, the reader may perhaps sense
from time to time that something more is here than generic
spiritual uplift. A Person is present in biblical preaching who is

able to take over the preacher, overriding human deficiencies. This Person is Himself the Word of God speaking by the Spirit through the flawed medium—the cracked pottery vessel often referred to in the Bible as an image of those whom God calls to convey the gospel. The poetic gift of George Herbert, using a different metaphor, not only strengthens the preacher but also teaches the hearer what happens in the pulpit:

> Lord, how can man preach thy eternal word?
>   He is a brittle crazie glass;
> Yet in thy temple thou dost him afford
>   This glorious and transcendent place,
>   To be a window, through thy grace.[6]

I have thought about what I might say to those who will use this book. It has been a curious exercise to imagine my sermons being read by an individual person as an act of devotion. It is often noted that sermons are intended for the ear, not the eye, and yet sermons by long-ago preachers like Augustine and John Donne are still read wherever there are Christian disciples. My sermons are not, of course, in that category, but as I write this introduction, I hope and pray that something of the sacred fire might still emerge from the page. Laura Bardolph Hubers is a person of discernment, and if she has hopes of this happening, it may be so! Most of all I wish for these sermons to be of help to those seeking to be formed deeply by the Word of God. I have not always been the best expositor that I wished to be, but I trust that the depth of my conviction about the power of the Word to create *ex nihilo*—out of nothing—will come through in ways beyond my comprehension.

I am particularly glad that Laura chose to arrange these selections according to the church calendar. A happy surprise in recent years has been the greatly increased interest in the liturgical year that is growing in Christian communities that lost it after the Reformation. If I may say so, the Church of

England, including my own branch of the Anglican Commu-
nion, the Episcopal Church, has been for four hundred years
the Protestant tradition most particularly devoted to the ob-
servance of the seasons of the church year.[7] Many people seem
to be talking about "formation" these days; I am not always
sure what they are referring to, but if there is one thing in addition to the Bible and the 1928 Book of Common Prayer that
has "formed" me, it is the church calendar. One of the gifts and
missions of the church is to resist the works of the devil; observing the seasons of the liturgical year is a particularly potent
way of resisting the overwhelmingly commercial rhythms and
demands of life in our present day, including the lies we tell
ourselves about self-creation. Advent and Lent are particularly
important as antidotes to the insistent demands of advertising
and cultural trends of every kind, but every date and season
in the church calendar teaches the life, death, and future coming of the risen Christ, and that in itself is formative. When
we reorient ourselves to the story of the God of Israel in Jesus
Christ, we participate in the life of God, and other claims to our
allegiance lose their power.

One of the "common prayers" in the 1928 Book of Common
Prayer is the General Thanksgiving, which is dear to the hearts
of all who grew up saying it in unison in Morning and Evening
Prayer. It includes this sentence:

> We bless thee for our creation, preservation, and all the bless-
> ings of this life, but above all, for thine inestimable love in
> the redemption of the world by our Lord Jesus Christ; for the
> means of grace, and for the hope of glory.

My only new contribution to this volume besides this introduction is this title: *Means of Grace*. Among all the gifts of God
to his people, the means of his Word faithfully preached and
faithfully heard is surely one of the greatest and most sure.

This introduction may or may not be a valediction on my

part, but if this volume is of some lesser or greater help to those whom the living Lord is presently calling to himself, it will have served its purpose.

Now may the God of peace who brought again from the dead our Lord Jesus, the great shepherd of the sheep, through the blood of the everlasting covenant, make you perfect in every good work to do his will, working in you that which is well-pleasing in his sight, through Jesus Christ, to whom be glory for ever and ever. Amen. (Heb. 13:20-21)

FLEMING RUTLEDGE
Penledge
Alford, Massachusetts

ADVENT

Mark 13:33–37

"Take heed, watch; for you do not know when the time will come."

—MARK 13:33

It is dark early at this time of year, and that reminds us of a darkness in our world. There is Christmas tinsel in the streets and Christmas music on the radio, but there is a cheapness at the core. The clock on the bank says it is day, but the hands on the church clock point to midnight.

It is Advent—the deepest place in the church year.

Advent—for the world, it is a time of counting shopping days before Christmas. Advent—for the church, it is the season of the shadows, the season of "the works of darkness," the season in which the church looks straight down into its own heart and finds there . . . the absence of God.

Now. Come back with me into the very first century AD when the Gospel of Mark was being put together. The young Christian church is going through a crisis of identity. It hears mocking laughter outside, voices saying, "Where is your King? You thought he was coming back, but he has not returned. You have made a very stupid mistake. How can you live without your Lord? He has abandoned you—for this, you want to risk your lives?"

And in its perplexity, the young church repeated a story to itself, a story once told by Jesus of Nazareth. It is one of the so-called crisis parables. It is the Gospel for the first Sunday in Advent, the parable of the doorkeeper.

There is a great household with many family members and many servants. There is a master, who established the household in the first place and gave it its reason for being; he is the one who gathered its members and assigned a place to each. It is he who put the whole operation in motion, who gave shape and direction to its existence. The master has gone away, but his orders are that there is to be a watch at the door, a constant alert. This is the command to the doorkeeper—"Stay awake"— but what he has said to the doorkeeper he says to everyone: "Keep awake." This state of readiness is to be maintained through the ceaseless vigilance of each family member and servant, each in his own work, until the master returns.

Perhaps you begin to feel the tension in the atmosphere of this parable. Were it not for the master, the household would have no reason for existing; yet he is away. The expectation of his return is the moving force behind all the activity that takes place; yet no one knows when the return will be. Everybody has been ordered to keep awake; yet the days and months and years pass, and still he does not come. Over and over again, the household repeats to itself the charge that it was given—"If he comes suddenly, he must not find us asleep."

The heartbeat of the parable is strong and accelerated—it is a parable of crisis. It is the story of the church, living in a crisis for two thousand years. The church calendar is not the same as the world's calendar. The Advent clock points to an hour that is later than the clock on the bank. There is knocking at the door! Take heed, watch—your Lord and Master may be standing at the gates this very moment. Keep awake, for if he comes suddenly, he must not find you asleep. "A thousand ages in his sight are like an evening gone."[8] There is no way for the church to adjust its calendar to the world's calendar.

The church is not part of contemporary culture, and never should have been. The church keeps her own deep inner rhythms. New Testament time is different from the world's time; Saint Paul says, "My friends, the time we live in will not last long.... For the whole frame of this world is passing away" (I Cor. 7:29, 31). New Testament time is a million years compressed into a single instant—and the time is *now*. "The hour cometh, and now is" (John 4:23). There is no way to alleviate the overwhelming tension produced by the Advent clock; the only way to be faithful is to be faithful at each moment. "Keep awake, for you do not know when the master of the house is coming."

The church lives in Advent. That is to say, the church lives between two advents. Jesus Christ has come; Jesus Christ will come. We do not know the day or the hour. If you find this tension almost unbearable at times, then you understand the Christian life. We live at what the New Testament depicts as the turn of the ages. In Jesus Christ, the kingdom of God is in head-on collision with the powers of darkness. The point of impact is the place where Christians take their stand. That is why it hurts. That's why the church has to take a beating. This is what Scripture tells us. No wonder there are so many who fall away; the church is located precisely where the battle line is drawn.

It is the Advent clock that tells the church what time it is. The church that keeps Advent is the church that is most truly herself. The church is not supposed to be prosperous and comfortable and established. It is Advent—it is dark and lonely and cold, and the master is away from home. Yet he will come. Keep awake.

He came among us once as a stranger, and we put him on a cross. He comes among us now, in the guise of the stranger at the door. He will come in the future, not as a stranger, but as the King in his glory, and "at the name of Jesus every knee should bow" (Phil. 2:10). "The coming of the Lord is at hand," says Saint James. "Behold, the Judge is standing at the doors" (James 5:8–9). Keep awake, then ... if he comes suddenly, he must not find you asleep.

PRAYER

Almighty God, give us grace that we may cast away the works of darkness, and put upon us the armor of light, now in the time of this mortal life in which thy Son Jesus Christ came to visit us in great humility; that in the last day, when he shall come again in his glorious majesty to judge both the quick and the dead, we may rise to the life immortal; through him who liveth and reigneth with thee and the Holy Ghost, one God, now and for ever. *Amen.*

....

Matthew 3:1, 7–10

"Even now the axe is laid to the root of the trees; every tree therefore that does not bear good fruit is cut down and thrown into the fire."

—MATTHEW 3:10

I t would be hard to say which is more alien to our contemporary ideas of getting ready for Christmas, the season of Advent or the figure of John the Baptist. All around the world, words are being read in churches that seem ill-suited, to say the very least, to the anticipated holidays. "You brood of vipers! Even now the axe is laid to the root of the trees!" How would you like to get that on a Christmas card? But there it is; this is the second Sunday of Advent, and the spotlight is on John the Baptist.

John the Baptist sets the tone for the first weeks of Advent, and in all four Gospels he sets the tone for the proclamation of Jesus Christ. Jesus arrives on the scene precisely at the moment John says, "Every tree that does not bear good fruit will be cut down and thrown into the fire." This is apocalyptic language, and it signifies the arrival of God.

When John said, "Repent, for the kingdom of heaven is at hand," his whole being, his entire existence, was on fire with the reality of the One Who Comes. He was in the grip of what I've been calling apocalyptic transvision—that vision given to the church that sees through the appearances of this world to the blazing power and holiness of the coming of the Lord.

John the Baptist is the ultimate embodiment of the apocalyptic character of Christian faith—faith that is oriented not to the past but to the future, not to the repetition of religious exercises but to the person of the Messiah, not to arrangements as they are but to an utterly new authority and dominion.

John stands at the very precipice of the collision of two forces, at the juncture where the world's resistance to God meets the irresistible force of the One Who Is Coming—"the axe is laid to the root of the trees." There he is, and there he will be until the trump sounds, forever summoning us to rethink and reorder our lives totally, orienting ourselves to an altogether new perspective—the perspective of God.

Have you recently considered the call to look at yourself the way God sees you? Does God care if you have a matched set of Gucci luggage? Will God judge you by the degree of recognition given to your name when it appears in the playbill, or on the letterhead, or in the list of trustees and patrons? Will he even judge you by your performance as a mother, or a husband, or a friend, or a neighbor? What will he judge you by?

Repent, for the kingdom of heaven is at hand.

Bear fruit that befits repentance.

Every tree that does not bear good fruit is cut down.

The criterion of judgment is the fruit that is characteristic of repentance. Is there anyone reading who needs to be reminded that repentance does not mean just being sorry? The Greek word *metanoia* means to turn around, to reorient oneself in another direction. It means to receive a new start altogether.

If I am told, over and over, to repent, to change, to orient my life to God, nothing will ever happen. I will cling to the earthly status symbols more desperately than ever. I don't need to hear exhortations to repent. I need power from outside myself to make me different.

A power from outside is coming, a power that is able to make a new creation out of people like us, people who have no capacity of ourselves to save ourselves. The power that is coming is not our power—not the power of our deeds, or our inner strength, or our spiritual discipline, or our faith, *or even our repentance.* It is God's power that gives good deeds and inner strength and spiritual discipline and faith and repentance. We are able to repent and bear fruit because he is coming.

What does it all mean?

It means any number of things. It means that you are being changed and I am being changed. It means that we Christians are going to be weaned away from our possessions and oriented toward being everlastingly possessed by the love of God. It means that we will become less interested in receiving personal blessings for ourselves and more interested in making Christian hope known to those who "sit in darkness." It means that we will become more and more thankful as we become less and less self-righteous. It means that we will gradually become less preoccupied with our own privileges and prerogatives and gradually see ourselves more and more in solidarity with other human beings who, like us, can receive mercy only from the hand of God and not because of any human superiority. Repentance will mean seeking after the good of all, not just the comforts of a few.

I said at the beginning that the Advent spotlight was on John the Baptist. Now it's time to revise that description. The spotlight is not on John; John himself *is* the spotlight. You probably haven't seen a spotlight unless you've been backstage. What you see is the beam of light and the object that is illuminated. John himself disappears; his preaching is the beam, and the light falls upon Jesus only. Yet even this simile fails us, because, as the Fourth Evangelist writes, "There was a man who came from God; his name was John. . . . He himself was not the light; he came only as a witness to the light" (John 1:6, 8).

The witness is from God; the light is from God; the preaching is from God—all for the purpose of revealing Jesus— Emmanuel, God-with-us. The preacher is nothing; the Word is everything. Jesus is everything. He comes; he comes at the end of the ages, and he comes in the hearts of all human beings who even now relinquish all human claims in the face of the God who is coming in power.

PRAYER

Merciful God, who sent thy messengers the prophets to preach repentance and prepare the way for our salvation: Give us grace to heed their warnings and forsake our sins, that we may greet with joy the coming of Jesus Christ our Redeemer; who liveth and reigneth with thee and the Holy Spirit, one God, now and for ever. *Amen.*

John 1:19–34

"Behold, the Lamb of God, who takes away the sin of the world!"

—JOHN 1:29

E very year in Advent, John the Baptist gets two whole Sundays to himself. We must recognize that this fire-breathing prophet, so very much the center of the Advent season, brings a message that is not at all what most people associate with Christmas. John's importance is not related to baby Jesus. John sees Jesus as an adult. He was destined to spend his entire life devoted to the single mission of announcing the arrival of the Messiah, and to prepare the people for his coming. For this devotion, he was locked in a dungeon and then brutally executed by the king and the first lady of Judea. Such is the cost of telling truth to power.

In all three Synoptic Gospels (Matthew, Mark, and Luke), John's message has two parts: *First,* he issues an uncompromising condemnation of the people for their sin—their greed, heedlessness, dishonesty, neglect of the poor, and above all, their easy assumption that God is on their side (Matt. 3:9; Luke 3:8). And *second,* he brings a fiery call to repentance and baptism for the remission of sin.

The Fourth Gospel, of John the Evangelist, usually presents things a bit differently. In this gospel, John the Baptist is the one who identifies Jesus by announcing, "*Behold, the Lamb of God, who takes away the sin of the world.*" This central affirmation is a particularly distinctive part of the message of John the Baptist. Yet sin plays no part in the run-up to Christmas as we know it in our culture today, and most people, even in the churches, have no idea what a Lamb of God might be except that it sounds sweet and fuzzy. In fact, John's salutation is a reference to Jesus's sacrificial death. In his death, Christ makes himself the substitute for the lambs that were slaughtered in the Old Testament rites, becoming the "full, perfect and sufficient sacrifice, oblation and satisfaction" for sin.[9] We don't hear about this kind of Lamb on Christmas cards. That's why we need Advent.

John's father, Zechariah, glorified the mission of the coming Messiah in these words:

> "The dayspring from on high hath visited us,
>   To give light to them that sit in darkness and in the
>   shadow of death." (Luke 1:78–79)

Now this doesn't mean "darkness and the shadow of death" in the general sense that "everybody has to die sooner or later." The images are much more textured than that. Darkness and the shadow of death are poetic images for our tragic, fallen human condition. "Dayspring" is also a poetic image, another name for the Messiah. "Dayspring" means something far more than just "dawn." It means the primordial source of day, God himself—the one who in the beginning said, "Let there be light." So when we read that the light dawns for those who suffer darkness and death (and that means all of us), it means that God is going to restore his original creation—but this time without the temptation of the serpent.

It's important for us to meditate deeply on *the darkness and the shadow of death* that we find ourselves in right now, as individuals, as a community, as a nation. The meaning of the season is not arguing about whether nativity scenes can be set up in the town park. The meaning of the season is *understanding why and how we sit in darkness* and *recognizing that we need to repent of our sinful nature.* That's what Advent is for. The Messiah is on his way.

The prophecies of Isaiah have always been associated with the Christmas season. But if you look in your Bible, you will see that the series of glorious promises often read in chapter 65 is immediately preceded by words that sound more like John the Baptist. This is the word of God to his people:

> [You are] a rebellious people,
> who walk in a way that is not good,
>   following their own devices;
> a people who provoke me
>   to my face continually....
> These are a smoke in my nostrils,
>   a fire that burns all the day....
> ... "I will repay ...
>   their iniquities and their fathers' iniquities together,
>   says the Lord." (Isa. 65:2-3, 5-7)

If we ignore passages like this—in other words, if we jump straight to Christmas without observing Advent—we will fail to understand the nature of the grace of God that comes to us even though we "provoke God to his face continually." Advent teaches us to recognize this grace, to turn aside from our own devices, and to wait in the darkness with patience for the promised time of fulfillment.

To be sure, Christmas is itself the time of fulfillment. The promised Messiah has appeared on earth. Yet the manner of his coming—in poverty, in obscurity, in humility—points ahead to the destiny that he will suffer on the cross.

This third Sunday of Advent, I bring you news of a living reality that changes everything. Jesus has come; Jesus will come. Whatever your own personal darkness, it has been and will be overcome. If you are not patient, God will yet grant you patience. If you are not charitable, the Savior will create charity in you. If you are not forgiving, the Lord will work a wonder of forgiveness in you. The darkness has been overcome, and it will be overcome.

There is always an element, in Advent, of "not yet." Not yet, but it will come. It will come because *he* will come. That is the promise given to us by God himself. The one who comes to be our Judge is the one who is the Lamb who takes away the sin of the world. The Lord *has* come and will come "to give light to them that sit in darkness and in the shadow of death" (Luke 1:79).

Behold, God creates a new heaven and a new earth.

PRAYER

Stir up thy power, O Lord, and with great might come among us; and, because we are sorely hindered by our sins, let thy bountiful grace and mercy speedily help and deliver us; through Jesus Christ our Lord, to whom, with thee and the Holy Ghost, be honor and glory, world without end. *Amen.*

....

2 Peter 3:8–15a

Since all these things are thus to be dissolved, what sort of persons ought you to be in lives of holiness and godliness, waiting for and hastening the coming day of God, because of which the heavens will be kindled and dissolved, and the elements will melt with fire!

—2 PETER 3:11–12

As a general rule, Americans are a people of action. We think of ourselves as busy, busy, busy making things happen, and we are a bit impatient with those who aren't full of energy as we are. We don't like passivity. We don't like waiting around. So the theme of *waiting and watching* that permeates the Advent season strikes a false note with us. We give lip service to it, but we don't take it very seriously. We don't want to sit around watching and waiting. We want to move things along. If God isn't going to bring the kingdom, we'll bring it ourselves.

I don't mean this lightly; I think we need to ask ourselves seriously, what are we going to do with this tiresome Advent refrain about watching and waiting? We hear it again in today's reading from the Second Epistle of Peter. The Bridegroom has been delayed. The Master is a long time coming, a lot longer than we expected. Shouldn't we forget about the theme of the second coming of Christ and get on with the job ourselves?

Advent is not really the season of preparing for Jesus's birth, as though he had never come in the first place. Advent is the season of preparation for his coming again.

And so, we come to our passage today from 2 Peter, with its fascinating pair of matched but opposing words: "Since all these things [everything mortal and perishable] are thus to be dissolved, what sort of persons ought you to be in lives of holiness and godliness, waiting for and hastening the coming of the day of God, because of which the heavens will be kindled and dissolved, and the elements will melt with fire! But according to his promise we wait for new heavens and a new earth in which righteousness dwells."

Waiting and hastening! How can you wait and hasten at the same time? That is the secret of the Christian life, knowing how to keep those two modes in creative tension, *"waiting for and hastening the coming of the day of God … [the] new heavens and a new earth in which righteousness dwells."* This is so typical of Advent, the time of contrasts and opposites: darkness and light, good and evil, past and future, now and not-yet.

Finding the right balance between *waiting* and *hastening* is the challenge of our existence in the body of Christ until he comes again. We might call it "action in waiting." The action part, the hastening part, is easy for us. That we understand. Tear down that old building, open up the new branch, build a new parking garage, start a new ad campaign, test the latest brand. The hard part is this waiting. What is the point of waiting? What are we waiting for? Why not get on with whatever it is?

Whatever it is, is this: "new heavens and a new earth in which righteousness dwells"; and no one can bring that about except God. Every year the Christmas cards go out, "Peace on Earth," and maybe we Americans can fool ourselves that there can be such a thing, but that would be to ignore the fact that three-fourths of the world's population is living in misery. The waiting of the Christian church, therefore, is the waiting and longing and hoping expressed in the haunting cry at the very end of the Bible: *"Maranatha:* Come, Lord Jesus" (Rev. 22:20).

Not until the final intervention of God in the last day will

the true and lasting peaceable kingdom come. That is the not-
yet of Advent. That is why we wait.

We come to our climactic question. If only God can bring
peace and good will, if only God can create "new heavens and
a new earth in which righteousness dwells," then what is the
point in our doing anything? If there's nothing we can do to
improve the situation, then we really might as well withdraw
into a private world of gated communities, exclusive clubs, and
personal privilege and enjoy it as best we can before we are
overtaken by cancer or senility.

Here's where the "action in waiting" comes in, the "hastening." It's all a matter of what we're pointing toward. Let's
look for a moment at another section of 2 Peter. Speaking of
the promises of God, the apostolic writer says, "We have the
prophetic word made more sure. . . . Pay attention to this as
to a lamp shining in a dark place, until the day dawns and the
morning star rises in your hearts" (2 Pet. 1:19). There's the Advent message, right there.

The church responds by doing the works of the day, the
works of the light, the ministry to the prisoners, the soup and
sandwiches for the hungry, the houses for the low-income
families, the birthday parties for the children who have no parties. These are lamps shining in dark places. These are works
that glorify Christ while we wait for him. This is action while
waiting.

We all stand on the threshold of God's kingdom. The Lord is
still out in front of us. His future still approaches, his future in
which all will be made new. His promise is sure; he will come.
We make ready for him, this Advent season and every season,
by lighting whatever little lights the Lord has put in front of us,
no light too small to be used by him, action in waiting, pointing ahead, looking to Christ and for Christ. Even our smallest
lights will be signs in this world, lights to show the way, beachheads to hold against the Enemy until the day when the great
Conqueror lands with Michael the archangel at the head of his

troops, the day that *shall dawn upon us from on high, to give light to those who sit in darkness and in the shadow of death, to guide our feet into the way of peace* (Luke 1:78–79).

PRAYER

We beseech thee, Almighty God, to purify our consciences by thy daily visitation, that when thy Son Jesus Christ cometh he may find in us a mansion prepared for himself; through the same Jesus Christ our Lord, who liveth and reigneth with thee, in the unity of the Holy Spirit, one God, now and for ever. *Amen.*

CHRISTMAS

Luke 1:26–38

"He will reign over the house of Jacob for ever;
and of his kingdom there will be no end."

—LUKE 1:33

I remember an image from years ago when I found myself, one deep December night just before Christmas Eve, driving through a very depressed, dark, and deserted neighborhood in Stamford, Connecticut. The street-level warehouses and other buildings were barred, bolted, or boarded up. The second- and third-story windows were empty, dingy, black. I had seen such neighborhoods many times before, of course, but for some reason, on this particular night, the darkness and emptiness of the streets seemed to me particularly oppressive and disturbing, and I locked my car door, as if to shut the feelings out.

Then, as I approached a deserted intersection, I looked up and saw among all those blank and lifeless windows one tiny string of multicolored Christmas lights, just one little string, hung across one window, bravely blinking out its message in the dark. Who knows who hung it there? Who knows what forlorn hope, what inarticulate longing, what simple human impulse of cheerfulness or defiance or humor or tenacity or courage caused it to appear in that window? I will never know; but it spoke to my heart, and I have not forgotten it to this day.

I think there is one thing clear amidst all the protests every year about the excess and the commercialism and the frenzy and the too-much-ness: even the most jaded of us will at some point let the truth slip—we need a little Christmas.

One year when my niece was seven years old, I took her to see *The Nutcracker* at Lincoln Center. Did I do that for my niece's benefit? No; it was really for me. One of the reasons for the enduring popularity of *The Nutcracker* is that it permits the grown-ups an evening of unadulterated Christmas magic on the pretense of taking the children.

Christmas magic. What is it? Not so much about Christmas trees that grow and snowflakes that dance, though that is an important part of the aura; no, the moment in the ballet that makes this grown woman choke up, year after year, is the part where evil is defeated conclusively and forever, the part where the little boy and little girl, holding hands, begin their magical journey through the enchanted forest, together, unafraid, the danger over and past, the phantoms banished, led and protected by a splendidly luminous star, into a kingdom of joy and delight where no disappointment can ever enter.

Magic is what we want; the illusion of magic puts billions of dollars in motion every December as we give permission to the advertisers and the retailers and the entertainers and the restaurants to let us pretend for a few weeks that there really is such a thing as magic, even though we know, we *know* there isn't.

One image is all it takes to shatter the illusion. I saw it in the paper recently—two young boys, in Ethiopia, wrapped in ragged blankets, bent almost double with the pain of starvation, their faces contorted into what looked like the most terrible smiles—the gruesome grimace of famine. Where is the magic?

There is no magic, really. We can send Christmas cards about love and peace all we want, but the human race is utterly incapable of turning itself around. The children who go to see *The Nutcracker* grow up to be victims of disappointment just like all the rest of us. There is no magical kingdom anywhere.

In a world no better and no worse than this one, at another time and in another place, where men and women struggled against poverty and disease and greed and disillusionment as we do, in a time when moments of hope and happiness and peace were just as delusory and fugitive as they are today, Saint Luke the Evangelist wrote a magical story.

> In the sixth month [of Elizabeth's pregnancy] the angel Gabriel was sent from God to a virgin [whose] name was Mary ... and the angel said to her, "Do not be afraid, Mary: for ... behold, you will conceive in your womb and bear a son, and you shall call his name Jesus. He will be great, and will be called the Son of the Most High; and the Lord God will give to him the throne of his father David ... and of his kingdom there shall be no end."
>
> And Mary said to the angel, "How can this be, since I do not know a man?" And the angel said to her, "The Holy Spirit will come upon you, and the power of the Most High will overshadow you; therefore the child to be born will be called holy, the Son of God ... for with God, nothing will be impossible."

An angel and a virgin. A heavenly messenger, an obscure young woman, a child who will be the Son of God. Gabriel comes to announce God's mighty reversal of the sin of the ancestors. He comes to proclaim the advent of the one who will save his people from their sins—a Savior, who is Christ the Lord.

This is the real magic. An angel and a virgin. God has acted. God has intervened. God is the one who rules over the everlasting kingdom that he delivers to his Son. In the announcement of Gabriel to the Virgin Mary, we hear a voice from beyond ourselves, a voice quite literally from out of this world. Only God is able to give true and lasting peace. Only God can create a new kingdom where no evil and no disappointment can ever enter.

The news from Saint Luke is that God himself has entered this world. His own blood will be shed in order to guarantee that the suffering in this world will one day come to an end forever. Jesus Christ, the Lord, is our hope. Jesus Christ is our future. Jesus, our Savior, and our God. The little strings of lights in the dark places remain lit, by his grace, until he comes again.

PRAYER

O God, who hast caused this holy night to shine with the illumination of the true Light: Grant us, we beseech thee, that as we have known the mystery of that Light upon earth, so may we also perfectly enjoy him in heaven; where with thee and the Holy Spirit he liveth and reigneth, one God, in glory everlasting. *Amen.*

Matthew 2:13–23

> "A voice was heard in Ramah,
> wailing and loud lamentation,
> Rachel weeping for her children;
> she refused to be consoled,
> because they are no more."

—MATTHEW 2:18

Every year at Christmastime I am amazed anew at the powerful hold on people's imaginations that the nativity story has. Everybody seems to like it. An acquaintance of mine who is stubbornly agnostic says that he reads it to himself every Christmas, but he does it in the bathroom where his atheist wife won't see him.

For most people in post-Christian America, the pulling power of the narrative is probably sentimental and nostalgic. It is therefore more important than ever for those who take Christian faith seriously to be aware of the deep and far-reaching claims the story actually makes.

The fourth day of Christmas is Holy Innocents Day, and the appointed reading for this Sunday is the story of Herod and his plan to get rid of the infant Jesus before he can grow up to become a threat. The Holy Family is wonderfully preserved by God, who sends them down to Egypt, but there is a wholesale massacre of baby boys back in Judea. This gruesome story is set right into the drama of the nativity by Saint Matthew, and the church from time immemorial has insisted on it as part of the Christmas celebration.

The key verse in Matthew's telling of this event is a quotation from the Old Testament: "What was said through the prophet Jeremiah is fulfilled: 'A voice is heard in Ramah, wailing and loud lamentation, Rachel weeping for her children, refusing to be comforted, because they are no more.'"

What does that make you think of? It makes me think of a remarkable speech by Geoffrey Canada, who heads an agency that serves poor children. Here is just one paragraph:

> Our children face monsters who kill in the night and the day, monsters who lurk in the dark. They see monsters on their way to school, in the park, in the hallways at night—monsters who leave traces of their brutal work, staining floors and walls, the vestiges of which tell of horrors unspeakable to such young minds. Our children know that we cannot see the monsters, not really, because if we saw them we would certainly protect them. What group of men and women would sacrifice their children to monsters?

This is the time for looking at monsters and naming them. This is the time to entertain seriously the arguments against believing the Christmas story. Ivan Karamazov in Dostoevsky's novel said that belief in God was not worth the suffering of even one child. We must listen to this objection again and again.

I took my mother to church on Christmas morning one year, and we sang the familiar carols. As we were driving home after the service, suddenly she said, "'Joy to the world, the Savior reigns.' What on earth does that mean? The Savior doesn't reign. Just look at all the horrible things that are going on." That's an observation made to order for Holy Innocents Day. In our reading today, we come up against the fact that, in the Christmas story as in today's world, the angels and the monsters coexist.

If it were not for the Rachel passage, I believe the claims of the Christmas story would be unendurable. In that case, baby Jesus and the angels and shepherds would have no more significance than Frosty the Snowman. This Christmas and every Christmas, the Rachel passage says to us that we can't run away from the suffering of the world. The suffering of the world is part of the story.

Everybody knows Handel's *Messiah*, but I wish more people had an opportunity to hear Hector Berlioz's *L'Enfance du Christ*. It tells the story of the slaughter of the innocents and the flight into Egypt. Among its many wonders is its tender, wrenching, deeply moving description of the Holy Family as they undergo terrifying hardships as refugees. Think of it—Jesus was a refugee! Berlioz shows them fleeing from the tyranny of Herod, meeting with contempt along the way because they are Jews, almost starving to death, taken in at last by a family of compassionate heathen Ishmaelites.

It is the paranoia of King Herod that drives the Holy Family into exile. In a memorable portion of Berlioz's oratorio we hear Herod working himself up into a homicidal frenzy. Like many a tyrant, he is pathologically insecure, only too ready to undertake mass murder to shore up his own position. Like Pontius Pilate some thirty-two or thirty-three years later, he senses his own overthrow in the presence of Jesus. Like Pilate, like every tyrant, Herod knew better than God's own people that the reign of a Savior meant the end of his own.

The Christmas story is anchored to our lives and to the wickedness of this world by the grief of Rachel, "weeping for her children, refusing to be comforted, because they are no more." The authors of Scripture did not turn away from the unimaginable suffering of children. God the Father did not turn away. Jesus did not turn away. But we must keep Ivan Karamazov's protest in our minds every day. The nativity story might as well be about reindeer and snowmen for sure, if it has nothing to say about the small victims.

I believe that, by putting Rachel's lament at the heart of the Christmas story, Matthew has shown us how to hold on to faith and hope until the second coming. Only as we share in the prayers and the laments of bereaved families, not looking away, can we continue to believe that the Savior reigns even now in the faith and tenacity of all those who continue to stand for humanity in the face of barbarity. Only by attending to the horrors of this world can we continue to sing the words of that great eighteenth-century hymn writer Isaac Watts:

> He comes to make his blessings known
> Far as the curse is found.[10]

For only a faith forged out of suffering can say with conviction that the angels and monsters will not coexist forever, that the agonies of the victims will someday be rectified, and that the unconditional love of God in Jesus Christ will be the Last Word.

PRAYER

We remember today, O God, the slaughter of the holy innocents of Bethlehem by the order of King Herod. Receive, we beseech thee, into the arms of thy mercy all innocent victims; and by thy great might frustrate the designs of evil tyrants and establish thy rule of justice, love, and peace; through Jesus Christ our Lord, who liveth and reigneth with thee, in the unity of the Holy Spirit, one God, for ever and ever. *Amen.*

Ephesians 2:1–10

And you he made alive, when you were dead through the trespasses and sins in which you once walked.

—EPHESIANS 2:1–2

Very often—more often than not, in fact—the Christian faith is presented as a rather static two-party transaction in which God presents himself to us and then stands back and lets us decide what choices and responses we're going to make. The emphasis is on *us*—*our* projections, *our* strategies, *our* decisions. God may be looking on as an interested, caring, and indeed loving spectator, but still a spectator, observing us as we work out our jobs and our lives and our wars but withholding his involvement, allowing us our free will and watching to see how well we perform. If we make the right choices, God will then approve.

But that's not what the New Testament shows us, and in particular it is not what the Epistle to the Ephesians dramatizes. The New Testament story is not a two-party transaction; it is a *three*-part *cosmic drama* in which the enemy plays a colossal role—indeed, a very nearly dominant role. To see this, we look at our reading from Ephesians for today. As always in the Bible, the bad news about our condition is preceded by the good news. Here are the first words of the chapter: *And you he made alive.* God has already come to us with his gift of new and eternal life. That precedes everything else.

But then the apostle continues, laying out before us the true state of things in the world. Until God intervened with his gift of life, he writes, *you were dead.*

> You [and I] were dead through the trespasses and sins in which [we] once walked, following the course of this world, following the prince of the power of the air, the spirit that is now at work in the sons of disobedience. Among these we all once lived in the passions of our flesh, following the desires of body and mind, and so we were by nature children of wrath, like the rest of mankind. (Eph. 2:1–3)

The basic scenario here is that there is an Enemy arrayed against us. The "prince of the power of the air" is called *Satan* in Scripture. The figure of Satan is symbolic; this symbolism functions to show us that the Enemy of God is a personal intelligence possessed of an implacable will and an unrelenting purpose, far stronger than the will or purpose of any human being, far stronger indeed than the wills or purposes of all human beings put together. Matthew's story of the temptation of Christ dramatizes the unique power of the incarnate Son of God, the only human being able to go head-to-head against this Enemy and confound him.

The story told in Ephesians, and indeed in all the New Testament, is that there are three active agencies, not two—and the three are (1) God, (2) *all* (not just *some*) of humanity, and (3) the Enemy. As we have seen, the Enemy is called in Ephesians "the prince of the power of the air." This prince—this formidable ruling power—is also called (in Eph. 6) "the devil" who commands "principalities and powers," who leads the "rulers of this present darkness," who marshals the "spiritual hosts of wickedness in the heavenly places."

So any other human—Saddam Hussein or Adolf Hitler or anyone else—is not the Enemy at all, except in a very limited sense. Rather, he is in the grip of the greater Enemy. But here is the point: we are all equally susceptible to the real Enemy.

But God ... says Ephesians, and when you hear those two words, "but God," in the New Testament, tune in, because you are about to hear the good news:

> But God, who is rich in mercy, out of the great love with which he loved us, even when we were dead through our trespasses, made us alive together with Christ (by grace you have been saved), and raised us up with him, and made us sit with him in the heavenly places in Christ Jesus.... For by grace you have been saved through faith; and this is not your own doing, it is the gift of God. (2:4–6, 8)

The Enemy, you see, is too strong for us. Only by the grace of God are we brought "out of error into truth, out of sin into righteousness, out of sin into life."[11] We cannot do it for ourselves. It is "not our own doing, it is the gift of God—not because of works, lest any man should boast" (2:8–9).

Now, the question always arises at this point in the gospel story: If God has done it all for us, what is there for us to do? The very best answer is in the next verse of our text. "For we are [God's] workmanship, created in Christ Jesus for good works, which God prepared beforehand, that we should walk in them" (2:10). God has already prepared our good choices for us, and he has guaranteed that what we do *in Christ Jesus* cannot be undone by the Enemy.

The story told to us in Ephesians is above all a universal story. It is the story of the whole of humanity in all its unacknowledged inner conflicts, moral ambiguity, mixed motives, and uncontrollable passions. All human beings are "children of wrath." Unaided human beings cannot free themselves from the Enemy. As Paul exclaims in Romans, "Who will deliver us from this body of Death?" (Rom. 7:24). It has been done for us by God through Jesus Christ, who was triumphant over Satan on Satan's own turf. The Enemy has been overridden by the greater Power. God has accomplished something that we could never have accomplished. Sin and Death, those cosmic Powers of the Enemy of God, no longer have any final hold upon us. The one who holds the future of the human race is God, and God alone.

And therefore, as Winston Churchill said to the English in the Battle of Britain, "Let us brace ourselves to our duties." Let us confidently go forth to "do all such good works as God has prepared for us to walk in." The ultimate outcome, for *all* of us warring human beings, belongs to God. Thanks be to God. "We are his workmanship, created in Christ Jesus for good works, which God prepared beforehand, that we should walk in them."

PRAYER

O God, who didst wonderfully create, and yet more wonderfully restore, the dignity of human nature: Grant that we may share the divine life of him who humbled himself to share our humanity, thy Son Jesus Christ; who liveth and reigneth with thee, in the unity of the Holy Spirit, one God, for ever and ever. *Amen.*

EPIPHANY

....

Judges 6:1–23; Psalm 111:10; Luke 5:1–11

The fear of the Lord is the beginning of wisdom.

—PSALM 111:10

The combination of heavenly grace and earthly fear is one of the most powerful recurrent themes in Scripture. Sometimes the word "fear" in English means something more like "reverence" or "awe," but very often it means just plain "terror" or "dread." What's hard for us to understand today is that when "the fear of the Lord" came upon the people, something beneficial was happening, even though it was terrifying.

Today we have two readings about the fear of the Lord, one from the Old Testament and one from the New.

We start with Gideon, an untried young man of no distinction from a small Hebrew tribe, threshing wheat in a hidden spot, hoping to hide his meager yield from the Midianites. As he engages in this pedestrian activity, suddenly an angel of the Lord appears to him and says, "The Lord is with you, you mighty man of valor" (Judg. 6:12). I think this is supposed to be funny. Gideon is not in the least a mighty man of valor. He is just a kid, a nonentity. He has the good sense to recognize this himself, for he says to the angel, "My clan is the weakest in Manasseh, and I am the least in my family." But the Lord says to him, "But I will be with you, and you shall smite the Midianites as [if they were] one man" (6:15–16). Notice that, in the Old Testament, "the angel of the Lord" is equivalent to the

Lord himself. If the angel is present and speaking, the Lord is present and speaking.

Gideon does not quite believe that this is the Lord speaking to him. He asks the angel to wait while he goes inside and prepares an offering so that the angel can give him a sign that it really is the Lord. The angel displays amazing patience: he sits down under a tree and waits for Gideon to go inside and prepare a young goat for cooking, with wheat cakes and broth. When Gideon gets back to the tree, the angel is still there; this is meant to amaze us, that the Lord of Hosts would indulge Gideon by sitting around like this. Gideon puts his present of a meal on top of a rock, and the angel tells him to drench the food. Now come the special effects:

> Then the angel of the Lord reached out the tip of the staff that was in his hand, and touched the meat and the unleavened cakes; and there sprang up fire from the rock and consumed the flesh and the unleavened cakes; and the angel of the Lord vanished from his sight. Then Gideon perceived that he was the angel of the Lord; and Gideon said, "Alas, O Lord God! For now I have seen the angel of the Lord face to face." But the Lord said to him, "Peace be to you; do not fear, you shall not die." (6:21–23)

It's commonplace to hear people declare that "the fear of God" is an Old Testament notion that is out of place in the New. But in our lesson from the Gospel of Luke today, we see how wrong that is. Jesus tells Simon Peter and his fellow fishermen to go back out after a very disappointing night, and the catch of fish is so huge that the nets start breaking and the boat begins to take on water. When the men get back to shore, do they whoop it up as if they had just won the lottery? On the contrary. Peter falls on his knees before Jesus standing on the beach and says, "Depart from me, for I am a sinful man, O Lord." And Jesus says to Simon, "Do not be afraid; henceforth you will be catching men." And when they had brought their boats to land, they left everything and followed him (Luke 5:8–11).

Two stories: one about Gideon, one about Peter. God draws near to them both, and both are overcome with terror. At the instant of their fear, however, the word of the Lord comes: Do not be afraid, for I will be with you for the mighty tasks that lie ahead. Luke's story is a parallel to the epiphanies of YHWH in the Old Testament.

Grace is terrifying. God is opposed to us; he is opposed to our selfishness, greed, idolatry, cruelty, pettiness, pomposity, vanity, and self-deceit. Yet God is for us. He is for us in ways that we can scarcely imagine—indeed, could not imagine if he had not revealed his conquering love in Jesus Christ. It is the love that *not only* opposes all that is harmful in the beloved *but also* has power to make our resistance go up in flames like Gideon's meat and cakes. When God appears, we are filled with fear; but the fear is instantly removed by the enabling word "Fear not." The fear of God is the beginning of wisdom because the awareness of sin comes only to those who are already standing on the firm ground of their salvation. The fear of God is the beginning of wisdom because it cannot come about unless God is present with us and for us.

You and I are deep in sin. We clutch our privileges to ourselves and are increasingly indifferent to the suffering of others, puffed up with an exaggerated idea of our own importance, deficient in giving and—most damaging of all—deficient in receiving love. Yet at any moment, while we are about our mundane daily lives, cleaning our nets, threshing our wheat, doing our income tax, riding the subway, there may suddenly come an irruption of grace—an angel sitting under a tree, a catch of fish, a strain of music, a Valentine, a spurt of energy, unexpected forgiveness, fire leaping from the rock. Count yourself blessed if, when such moments come, you have a sensation of holy dread, a suspicion that what has happened might have

come *even though* you don't deserve it, an intimation that all
good things come not from within ourselves but as mercy
from above.

If your rebelliousness and mine were allowed to play themselves out to the end, we would be lost; but the God who terri-
fies is also the one who loves us for all eternity. If you come to
know the fear of the Lord, count yourself blessed, for the next
words that you hear will be

Fear not: for, behold, I bring you good tidings of great joy.

PRAYER

O God ... lead us, who know thee now by faith, to thy presence,
where we may behold thy glory face to face; through the same
Jesus Christ our Lord, who liveth and reigneth with thee and
the Holy Spirit, one God, now and for ever. *Amen.*

Isaiah 42:1–9

Behold, ... new things I now declare.

—ISAIAH 42:9

I remember a fascinating story I read once in the *New York Times* about homeless young people who panhandled by day and lived in the Port Authority Bus Terminal by night. The central characters in the article were a group of former crack addicts trying to get hold of a new start in life. One young woman was eager to prove that she had not stolen her little TV set. Offering to show the receipt for it, she said, "We are trying to turn ourselves around." There is something inside all of us, I think, that responds to this. We can understand and even admire the hope, however forlorn, for something better.

The worst thing of all, it seems to me, would be to be in a situation without hope of some kind. This hopelessness must have assailed the people of Israel during the time of the Babylonian exile in the fourth century BC. They had suffered the loss of home, loss of nation, loss of possessions, loss of the temple, loss of status, roots, traditions, customs, freedoms, identity, sense of belonging. The Babylonians were a great and powerful culture with many great and powerful gods who apparently were able to give mighty victories to their worshipers. Israel, a tiny little nation to begin with, would appear to be almost totally swallowed up by the rich, warmongering Babylonians; and, what was even more significant, Israel's god Yahweh seemed to have been completely stampeded by Marduk and the other Babylonian gods.

In this situation, the second prophet Isaiah carried out his ministry. His work comes down to us in chapters 40–55 of the book of Isaiah. In a situation of hopelessness, the prophet opens his ministry by addressing the people with these celebrated words of literally unimaginable promise:

> Comfort ye, comfort ye, my people,
>   saith your God.
> Speak ye comfortably to Jerusalem,
> and cry unto her,
>   that her warfare is accomplished,
> that her iniquity is pardoned,
>   that she hath received from the Lord's hand
> double for all her sins. (Isa. 40:1–2)

When it comes to the frontier of innovation, the vanguard, the state of the art, this prophet whom we call Second Isaiah is in a class by himself. God delivered messages to him that, for sustained sublimity and exaltation of vision, are unparalleled anywhere else.

> "From this time forth I make you hear new things,
>   hidden things which you have not known.
> They are created now ...
>   before today you have never heard of them." (48:6–7)

Notice the most radical announcement here. "Before today you have never heard of" the things that God will do. They are not accessible to human imagination. "They are created now." This feature of Second Isaiah is what has led interpreters to call this prophet the first apocalyptic theologian—meaning, the first to show in an unmistakable way that God will interrupt the normal progression of things by arriving in—indeed, invading—the midst of human events from a sphere of power capable of calling into existence the things that do not exist.

It is no accident that Isaiah 42 is read today. This is the day of the baptism of the Lord. Something is happening today that is so utterly new that the human brain cannot possibly have projected it. God has become man. Yahweh, the Holy One of Israel, the first and the last, who gives his glory to no other, has come down in the person of his Son to be dunked in the muddy waters of the Jordan River for the washing away of sin. Whose sin? Listen to these words:

> Surely he has borne our griefs
>   and carried our sorrows....
> All we like sheep have gone astray;
>   we have turned every one to his own way;
> and the Lord has laid on him
>   the iniquity of us all. (53:4, 6)

These words, so familiar to us from Handel's *Messiah*, take on an entirely new meaning when heard in their original context. At the climax of Second Isaiah's extended, rapturous, ecstatic vision of the paradise that God is going to create, in some of the most exalted language ever produced on paper, suddenly there appears the startlingly, wrenchingly, bafflingly disjunctive picture of what the church has always understood to be the crucified Christ.

The Epiphany season marks the transition from the manger to the cross. The ultimate glory of God is to be brought about by the ultimate sacrifice. Life is to be wrested from death; sin is to be conquered by the Son of God taking upon himself the sin of the world.

Here is an image. The young woman who lives in the Port Authority Bus Terminal has been a crack addict; she has lied, cheated, and stolen. When she is asleep in her blanket on the floor, there is no way for a passerby to know whether or not she is trying to kick her habit and better herself. Yet, according to the article, she constantly finds that bus passengers put a dollar bill or two, even on occasion a twenty-dollar bill, into her blanket while she is asleep.

Jesus stoops down to us in our miserable condition, bringing the gifts of new life. He does not ask us what we are doing to make ourselves better; he just gives the gift. He does not ask if we are working to turn ourselves around; he does not ask for a receipt; he puts redemption into our blanket. And, having done it, he does not then get on a bus and go to a warmer, more comfortable place; instead, with no place to lay his own head, he gives himself up to suffering and death, paying in his own body the price of sin, idolatry, addiction, greed, pride, and every form of human wickedness. In this sacrifice, toward which the church begins to move in Epiphany, there is a whole new world where everything is changed, where hope appears in the midst of hopelessness, where the promises of God break through to the exiles, where even the smallest acts of human charity signify the coming of the time when the dead will be raised, and all our sins and foolishness will be no more.

PRAYER

Father in heaven, who at the baptism of Jesus in the River Jordan didst proclaim him thy beloved Son and anoint him with the Holy Spirit: Grant that all who are baptized into his Name may keep the covenant they have made, and boldly confess him as Lord and Savior; who with thee and the same Holy Spirit liveth and reigneth, one God, in glory everlasting. *Amen.*

John 2:1–11

When the steward of the feast tasted the water now become wine, and did not know where it came from (though the servants who had drawn the water knew), the steward of the feast called the bridegroom and said to him, "Every man serves the good wine first; and when men have drunk freely, then the poor wine; but you have kept the good wine until now."

—JOHN 2:9–10

I often read the personal ads in magazines. Nowhere will you find a more comprehensive index of human longing. The wittiest and most literary ones are, predictably, in the *New York Review of Books.* Here is my all-time favorite:

> Reflecting over the past, it seems at mid-life that there's not much more time to search for dreams. Married man of means and mien looks for a woman who feels that there should have been more to it all. Age and marital status unimportant. Discretion assured.

That's an exceptionally poignant and candid summary of the regret at the heart of human life. I do not believe there is anyone today, however well defended, who does not recognize the creeping chill of that feeling—"there should have been more to it all." And when this feeling assails us, when this sense of having been deprived gnaws at us, we take refuge in all sorts of escapes; we buy something and charge it, we drink, we pop a pill, we grab for sexual adventure, we throw a lavish party, we read the latest self-help book or go to the guru of the moment.

In today's reading from John's Gospel, we discover Jesus at a wedding where the wine has run out. We can imagine the dismayed host saying, "Is that all there is?"

There's something else wrong at the wedding at Cana in Galilee. There are those water pots standing by for the Jewish rite of purification. They are "a reminder that all is not well and that there is a need greater than that of a further supply of wine."[12] Water from them is used for the washing away of sin. It is used, but it doesn't work. It is tasteless and colorless and joyless, and it doesn't take away sin. The Epistle to the Hebrews tells us that religious rituals "can never ... make perfect those who draw near.... In these sacrifices [these purifications] there is a reminder of sin year after year" (Heb. 10:1–3). The water in the story represents all our human attempts, and especially our religious attempts, to make things right.[13]

Jesus says, "Fill the jars with water." This is a big order. Each jar held 15 to 25 gallons, and there were 6 jars. At a minimum, then, we are talking about 90 gallons. Most scholars suggest at least 120 gallons. If there are 4 quarts to a gallon and each quart yields 6 glasses, that's a minimum total of 2,160 glasses. The servants, trusting Jesus, haul this huge amount of water and fill the jars. Jesus says, "Now draw some out, and take it to the steward of the feast."

The evangelist John is a great storyteller. He doesn't bore us by saying anything so pedestrian as "The steward tasted the water and discovered that it had turned into wine." Instead, the next thing we hear is the steward's exuberant shout to the host, congratulating him: "Everybody else I know puts the good wine out first and then when people's taste buds are shot, they bring out the cheap stuff. But you have kept back your good wine until now!"

I want you to feel this in your inmost being. What has Jesus done? Twenty-one hundred glasses of the finest vintage for one little wedding party in a backwater village! What does this mean? It is the Gospel of John that gives us Jesus's words, "I am come that they might have life, and that they might have it more abundantly" (10:10). The wine so freely given represents Jesus's gift of himself. Every Jew in Jesus's time knew that the wedding feast, throughout the Hebrew Bible, was the primary image of salvation, the banquet of redemption in the kingdom of God. And so when Jesus, *at a wedding*, poured out more good wine than anyone had ever seen, those who had eyes to see and ears to hear recognized that the future blessings of the heavenly kingdom had become present in the miracle of Jesus. "This," John writes, "the first of his signs, Jesus did at Cana in Galilee, and manifested his glory; and his disciples believed in him."

Jesus sees our predicament. He hears our news—*the wine has run out*, and we are still in our sins. He sees us, he sees our whole society, he sees the whole world full of disease and violence and cruelty and death, afflicted with conditions that religious rituals have never been able to improve. He sees us, he loves us, and he has come to pour out his life for us. The message of Christmas was that the Son of God is born among us. The message of Epiphany is that the Son of God is powerful to save. Whenever you find yourself asking, "Is that all there is?" remember: *no, it is not all*. There is the promise of God through faith in Jesus Christ, and that is everything.

And please understand this: the promise of Jesus does not refer only to some far-off future day. He gives his life to us now, not a life of conspicuous consumption ending in emptiness, but a life of service to others and to God's suffering world, a life that is built not on chasing dreams and fantasies, but being built by the Holy Spirit into a fellowship of love that gathers even now at the Lord's table. He, the only begotten, the Messiah of Israel, is the one, the only one who is able to give purification, the only one who is able to wipe away regret forever, the only one in whose name we find ourselves redeemed and restored and brought into an eternal future where there will be no need to search for dreams, because the dream of all humanity is summed up in the cross and in the resurrection of our Lord Jesus Christ. He goes to prepare a place for us at his own unending banquet. May he confirm this truth in your heart, today and forever.

PRAYER

Almighty God, whose Son our Savior Jesus Christ is the light of the world: Grant that thy people, illumined by thy Word and sacraments, may shine with the radiance of Christ's glory, that he may be known, worshiped, and obeyed to the ends of the earth; through Jesus Christ our Lord, who with thee and the Holy Spirit liveth and reigneth, one God, now and for ever. *Amen.*

1 Kings 18:20–19:18

And behold, the Lord passed by, and a great and strong wind rent the mountains, and broke in pieces the rocks before the Lord, but the Lord was not in the wind; and after the wind an earthquake, but the Lord was not in the earthquake; and after the earthquake a fire, but the Lord was not in the fire; and after the fire a still small voice.

—1 KINGS 19:11–12

There is more drama in the story of Elijah than that of almost any other biblical character. He was a mighty warrior for the Lord, and we get the impression that he enjoyed it. He loved it when God fully unleashed his might. He relished the whole idea of calling down fire upon the enemies of God, and he did just that, on Mount Carmel. When Elijah spoke the word, God sent down a thunderbolt and a great storm of rain, and Elijah was exultant.

After the great demonstration on Mount Carmel, the victory over Baal, and the massacre of the false prophets, Elijah's adrenaline was pumping. Flush with victory, he was ecstatic to think of how the whole nation had now been won for the Lord. Now the wicked queen Jezebel would at last bow down before the one God of Israel. How could God have made his message more plain than he had on the mountain? Surely now the people would return to the one who had redeemed them and forged them into a nation.

But, of course, that's not what happened. The mass conversion he was expecting did not occur; the fickle people went right back to Baal worship as if nothing had ever happened.

Elijah is experiencing a colossal comedown; his energy and courage have deserted him. So he goes off in a fit of gloom, lies down on the ground, and begs to die, since he hasn't been any more effective than the prophets before him. After all the fireworks on Carmel, God seems to have fizzled out. His enemies are as active as ever. Elijah feels there is nothing left for him to do.

The Lord is gentle with Elijah. Instead of reproaching him, the Lord sends an angel to feed him, encourage him, and strengthen him. Partly recovered, he pushes on to Mount Horeb, where he takes shelter in a cave. He doesn't know it yet, but the Lord has brought him on a retreat.

> And there he came to a cave, and lodged there; and behold, the word of the Lord came to him.... "What are you doing here, Elijah?" He [Elijah] said, "...The people of Israel have forsaken thy covenant, thrown down thy altars, and slain thy prophets with the sword; and I, even I only, am left; and they seek my life, to take it away." (19:9–10)

"Only I am left": notice that! How often we feel that way! Nobody is on my side! Nobody understands me! I haven't had any successes! I've knocked myself out for nothing! I've been abandoned! Moreover, Elijah fails to mention the prophets of Baal that *he* killed with the sword; he's focused on his own colleagues, whom *Jezebel* killed. He can't see past his own grandiosity. He thinks he's the only worshiper left in Israel. He has ceased to trust God. The Lord's great plan is no longer in his mind.

But again, the Lord is very good to Elijah. He has fed him, strengthened him, and spoken to him. And now God says, "Go forth, and stand upon the mount before the Lord." And behold, the Lord passed by, and a great and strong wind rent the mountains, and broke in pieces the rocks before the Lord (19:11). This, of course, is Elijah's favorite thing. But the Lord was not in the wind, or the subsequent earthquake, or the fire.

What a disappointment! Where are the special effects?

There is a major lesson here about the nature of God. The Bible teaches this lesson in many places, especially the Psalms. The Lord is the master of creation, but he is not "in" creation. The creation praises God, but it is not itself God; God is not "in" it. The sunset, the mountains, the lakes and rivers, the winds and storms, the mighty ocean and the creatures in it—the Lord God made them all, and they serve him, but they are not God; he is not "in" them.

Where is God, then?

God is in his Word.

The Lord was not in the wind, or the earthquake, or the fire. He came to Elijah another way, in "a still small voice." God does many things to prepare us to hear his Word. Sometimes he gets our attention with big displays, but far more often he wins our hearts and minds with a still, small voice. Sometimes people have "conversion experiences" at big rallies and revivals, but the initial power of such events cannot be sustained without the steady witness of the less flamboyant members of the faithful people of God—the Sunday school teacher, the greeter, the prayer-group leader, the simple, everyday believing Christian. The Holy Spirit blows where it wills.

In the Gospel of Luke, we read that the people of a Samaritan village refused to receive Jesus. The disciples James and John were seized by vengeful feelings. They said, "Lord, do you want us to bid fire to come down from heaven and consume them?" (Luke 9:54). That's just like Elijah, isn't it? Here's what the Lord said after James and John asked him if they could incinerate his enemies: "Foxes have holes, and birds of the air have nests; but the Son of man has nowhere to lay his head" (9:58). The Son of God, the incarnate Word, has not come in fire, or thunder, or great demonstrations of power. His power is of another sort. It is the power of the Creator of the world, but it is the power that steps away from power. It is the power that offers up God's self in suffering love: the still, small voice.

We may learn this lesson from Elijah today. There will be no fireworks as you read, no crashes of sermonic thunder, no oratorical displays. But the Lord is present here. He is present in the teaching of this biblical story because that is what he promised. He is present in the prayers of his people because that is what he promised. May we, so to speak, wrap our faces like Elijah—wrap our faces in thanksgiving, in adoration, in awe and in humility before the presence of the Lord.

PRAYER

Give us grace, O Lord, to answer readily the call of our Savior Jesus Christ and proclaim to all people the Good News of his salvation, that we and the whole world may perceive the glory of his marvelous works; who liveth and reigneth with thee and the Holy Spirit, one God, for ever and ever. *Amen.*

Isaiah 28

> *The Lord will rise up ...*
> *to do his deed—strange is his deed!*
> *and to work his work—alien is his work!*
>
> —ISAIAH 28:21

All my life I have been gripped by the problem of evil and suffering. These are the kinds of questions that disturb me and many other Christians:

- Why does God allow evil?
- Why do some people suffer so much while others seem to glide through life?
- Why do so many prayers go unanswered?
- If God is in control, why are so many things out of control?

More and more, as I have thought about these questions, I have been drawn to Isaiah 28.

The prophet Isaiah, who was an aristocrat born to privilege, could not have foreseen the kind of life God called him into. Instead of enjoying the comforts and privileges of upper-class life, Isaiah had to spend his entire adulthood preaching to the people about sin and judgment. Of course, that's not all he preached. It is no accident that Isaiah is the prophet of the Christmas season—his matchless messianic prophecies are among the glories of the Christian tradition.

But there can be no denying that Isaiah had a hard message to bring to the people. In a way, his message is no help to us in dealing with the problem of evil, because even though his preaching clearly commanded trust in the true God, the people had made "a covenant with death" (28:15), and they were "grinding the faces of the poor" (3:15). So the Assyrian invasion, which Isaiah warned against, was a logical consequence of Israel's disloyalty to her God.

But the prophet's words have a wider application. More and more, when I read and hear about awful things happening, I find myself thinking in the terms that Isaiah used. I'm speaking specifically of these verses:

> The Lord will rise up, as he did at Mount Perazim;
>   he will rouse himself, as in the valley of Gibeon,
> to do his work, his strange work,
>   and perform his task, his alien task. (28:21)

God's strange work, his alien work—these are terms that have proven to be theologically fruitful. Martin Luther drew upon this text to develop the idea that God has *proper work* (*opus proprium*) and *alien work* (*opus alienum*). The easiest and most picturesque way of talking about this is in terms of God's right hand and God's left hand. This imagery comes from the Old Testament also; throughout the Hebrew Bible, God's work of deliverance and salvation is referred to as the work of his strong right hand and his outstretched arm. So it makes sense to think of his work of judgment as the work of his strong left hand.

Now, it's interesting that God's right and left hands are perceived differently by different groups of people. In the book of Exodus, we have the wonderful poem called "The Song of Moses." Moses and the Israelites, having been delivered from Pharaoh's army at the Red Sea, sing a hymn of praise to God:

"Who among the gods is like you, O Lord?
Majestic in holiness, awesome in glory, working wonders—
you stretched out your right hand and the earth swallowed
up [the Egyptians]." (Exod. 15:11–12)

This is all very well from the standpoint of the Israelites,
but we can be sure that the Egyptians did not experience this
in the same way. We might say that, to the Egyptians, it is God's
left hand.

Studying the Bible and trying to make sense of it in our own
lives has been called "thinking God's thoughts after him." The
Bible is unique among books because it is written *from God's
point of view*. Let's pause over that for a moment, because it is a
staggering claim. That claim could not be made if it were not
for one conviction: *that God has truly revealed himself in his Word*.
If it is true, then the Bible—despite the assertions of a great
many textual critics and historians of religion—is written not
from the point of view of Israel or Egypt, Jew or gentile, but
from God's point of view. And God knows what he is doing
with his right hand and what he is doing with his left. We don't,
but he does. And it is God's right hand that does his proper
work, his ultimate work. His left hand is doing his *penultimate*
work, his alien work, the work of judgment that will finally be
taken up into his saving work, the work of his right hand.

This view, I know, raises many questions. We are not addressing the problem of radical evil today. It isn't possible in a
short space like this to go into all the vexed issues and distress-
ing convolutions. But taking this view has the great virtue of
allowing for the perplexity and grief and pain that are suffered
on all sides in times of disaster. It is much better than saying
either "This was God's will" or "God isn't in control."

Every one of you is either going to face these kinds of problems someday or is already facing them today. You are going
to wonder where God is, why he doesn't act, why he seems to
do the exact opposite of what you asked, why everything goes

wrong. You are going to ask why your most precious dreams burst like bubbles, why your fondest hopes vanished into the air, why your greatest enthusiasms evaporated into bitter disappointments.

I do not have an answer for these questions, but I do have a testimony. I believe it is better to be in God's left hand than in the devil's right. I believe it is better to trust the Lord's alien work than to give oneself over to the proper work of some other lord, some other god. I believe that our greatest sorrow and most excruciating pain are better delivered into the Lord's care than clutched angrily to oneself. He is God. He is righteous, and just, and merciful, and good, and someday we will see that he is. Several decades of wrestling with these questions have deepened my conviction that both of the Lord's hands can be trusted. For, as we read in Isaiah 28:29, all this also comes from the Lord almighty, wonderful in counsel and magnificent in wisdom.

PRAYER

Almighty and everlasting God, who dost govern all things in heaven and earth: Mercifully hear the supplications of thy people, and in our time grant us thy peace; through Jesus Christ our Lord, who liveth and reigneth with thee and the Holy Spirit, one God, for ever and ever. *Amen.*

Romans 4

The words, "it was reckoned to [Abraham]," were written not for his sake alone, but for ours also.

—ROMANS 4:23

I n the Hebrew tradition inherited by Jesus and Paul, the patriarch Abraham was considered the model of a man who was close to God. This inherited conception had several results. Abraham was idealized; his flesh-and-blood descendants came to regard themselves as distinct from others, possessing special righteousness. At the same time, Abraham's qualities of faith and holiness came to be regarded as human attainments, possible for some, impossible for many others.

It seems to me that we do this same number on our religious leaders today. We idealize them and are scandalized when their faults are revealed; we attach ourselves to them and draw a sense of self-regard from our proximity; we invest them with special spiritual powers. Sometimes we seek to imitate their lives, but at other times when we want to get off the hook, we think of them as being too far above us to aspire to.

All these attitudes are dead wrong, the apostle Paul is telling us. When we think of Abraham or Mother Teresa or our own clergy or anyone else as models of righteousness and godliness, it is a form of idolatry. Against this type of thinking Saint Paul writes: "There is no distinction" (Rom. 3:22), "There is no difference" (10:12). And in Romans 4, Paul picks the man who is called "the father of us all" (4:11) to illustrate his point. He selects the truly heroic figure of Abraham to demonstrate the unrighteousness and ungodliness of all mankind.

In Genesis 12, we are told that the Lord spoke to Abraham. This is what he said:

> "Go from your country and your kindred and your father's house to the land that I will show you. And I will make of you a great nation, and I will bless you and make your name great, so that you will be a blessing . . . and by you all the nations of the earth will be blessed."

This passage is usually identified as "Abraham's call." But did any of you notice, when you read Romans 4 just now, the thing that Paul noticed about that speech of the Lord's? Paul was struck by the fact that it was not only a *call* but also a *promise,* and that the promise was *unconditional.* There are no "ifs" in it. God didn't say to Abraham, *if* you're righteous I will bless you, or *if* you believe I will bless you, or *if* you repent I will bless you. He just said, "I will bless you." Period. And then he said that Abraham's descendants would be a blessing to all the peoples of the earth—all of them.

By the time of Saint Paul, being a child of Abraham had become a real status symbol, and a lot of conditions had been put on it. It was being taken for granted by many that children of Abraham were righteous and godly; they were "very religious" and "close to God," and this separated them from the common herd.

The first person in the New Testament to challenge this was John the Baptist, who shouted at the "religious" people who came to him, "Do not presume to say to yourselves, 'We are children of Abraham,' for I tell you, God is able to raise up children to Abraham from these stones" (Matt. 3:9). Paul takes up this theme in his own characteristic way in chapter 4 of Romans. Paul wants to show us, from the Old Testament, what the true foundation of righteousness and godliness is. Paul's message was shocking in his own time, and it is still shocking today, but for those who hear it and receive it, it is nothing less than life out of death.

Paul found a word in Genesis 15:6, and again in Psalm 32:2, that he made the centerpiece of his discussion of Abraham in Romans 4. The word is "reckon."

Paul doesn't use the word "reckon" the way Southerners use it. He uses it the way an accountant would if he were going to "reckon" up a column of figures. Quoting Genesis 15:6 from his Greek translation, Paul says that Abraham was righteous, not because he was faithful or obedient or godly, but because God "reckoned" him as righteous. It really is another way of saying that Abraham was not righteous, was not godly, indeed, that he was one of the ungodly until God reckoned him righteous. It is no longer possible to say that Abraham has anything to his credit. Credit comes to him as a pure, unearned gift from God. This is called grace.

This unilateral "reckoning" of God is God's action. Abraham did not get close to God; God came close to him. Abraham was not spiritually prepared for this; he was not possessed of any special religious consciousness. He was just an ordinary man who became extraordinary because God grabbed hold of him.

Now, what this means for us is that everything that separates us from each other is swept away. The heroic figures that seem so distant from us are sinners just like us; we sinners are justified and reckoned righteous just as they are. God is just as close to you as he is to those you most respect and admire, and just as able to work righteousness in your life as he is in their lives. This righteousness of God will take different forms in different lives, depending upon the dispensation of gifts as God chooses to bestow them, but, since it is his distribution, we are freed from anxiety about it.

Even as this wonderful news, this gospel, enters into our

hearts, however, the cry invariably goes up, "But does this mean we don't have to *do* anything?" As Paul puts it in Romans 6:1, "Are we then to continue in sin in order that grace may abound?" His answer to this is, "God forbid!" For those who have really felt the force of the divine reckoning, the new life in Christ can only take shape as an intense longing to do good instead of evil, to love mercy, to do battle against injustice, to serve God in the least of these his brethren.

And so may we today receive into our hearts the astonishing news that the Father on his throne of judgment in heaven has turned his face to us and, beholding us ungodly offenders through the eyes of his beloved Son, has said to us, "Your faith is reckoned to you as righteousness."

PRAYER

Set us free, O God, from the bondage of our sins, and give us, we beseech thee, the liberty of that abundant life which thou hast manifested to us in thy Son our Savior Jesus Christ; who liveth and reigneth with thee, in the unity of the Holy Spirit, one God, now and for ever. *Amen.*

SIXTH SUNDAY AFTER THE EPIPHANY

Jeremiah 17:5–10; 31:31–33

"This is the covenant which I will make with the house of Israel after those days, says the Lord: I will put my law within them, and I will write it upon their hearts; and I will be their God, and they shall be my people."

—JEREMIAH 31:33

The book of Jeremiah is very difficult to teach. I have taught almost every book of the Bible, and this is the only one that I felt I had to break up into various pieces according to themes, rather than taking it verse by verse. It just doesn't seem to have any logical progression from one chapter to the next. We think it was put together from various portions of the prophet's teaching over a period of decades, without much coherence. However, more and more in recent years I have come to believe that the shape of the book as we have it is part of the Holy Spirit's intention.

The passage we're looking at from chapter 17 today is an example. You'll see that the first two parts seem logically connected. The person who trusts in human potential instead of God's life-giving power is like a scrubby plant that can never thrive because it's in the desert. This is contrasted with the lovely image of the person who trusts in the Lord. Such a person is like a tree planted by an unfailing source of life-giving water.

But then Jeremiah suddenly says, "The heart is deceitful

59

above all things, and desperately corrupt; who can understand it?" This sweeping, all-inclusive statement doesn't seem to have any connection to the image of the thriving green tree by the stream. Moreover, he then goes on to transmit the Lord's warning: "I the Lord search the mind and try the heart, to give to every man according to his ways, according to the fruit of his doings." That makes me feel very uneasy. If the human heart is corrupt and deceitful beyond all things, and if God is going to assess everyone according to his or her doings, then what confidence can we have? The same indictment of the human heart appears in various other places in the Bible:

> The Lord saw that the wickedness of man was great in the earth, and that every imagination of the thoughts of his heart was only evil continually. (Gen. 6:5)

> The hearts of men are full of evil, and madness is in their hearts while they live, and after that they go to the dead. (Eccles. 9:3)

> God looks down from heaven
>   upon the children of men
> to see if there are any that are wise,
>   that seek after God.
> They have all fallen away;
>   they are all alike depraved;
> there is none that does good,
>   no, not one. (Ps. 53:2–3)

According to the Scripture, there is a vast disruption in the creation that has affected every human being ever born. The apostle Paul picks up this theme in Romans, citing Psalm 53: "There is no one righteous, no, not one" (3:10). This is a central teaching in biblical faith. We surround ourselves with all sorts of defenses against these bleak truths, but in our essential selves, we are dislocated; we are estranged; we are essentially alone; we "go to the dead."

The Bible's depiction of the human condition is ruthless and relentless. It is a long saga of idolatry, apostasy, chicanery, cowardice, incest, rape, violence, deceit, betrayal, murder, and the well-deserved judgment of God. It omits nothing.

And yet ... and yet.

We're going to leap over thirteen chapters and read one of the most important passages in all of Scripture. Let us hold in our minds the picture of the human heart, "deceitful above all things, and desperately corrupt." We are skipping over whole chapters describing the determination of the people to pursue their course of self-destruction. Remember the words "I the Lord search the mind and try the heart." Recall also the concluding words of our reading: God searches our hearts "to give to every person according to his ways, according to the fruit of his doings." Do you—do I—think we can stand up to that? I know I can't. We are up against a stone wall here. The human heart is desperately corrupt and beyond self-help. The history of biblical Israel proves it. The tabloids prove it. The nightly news proves it.

But now read Jeremiah 31:31–33—the new covenant passage. Here are the plan and purpose of God to overcome the resistance of the human heart. Here is the great action that the Lord is preparing to redeem his creation from its bondage to sin. Here are the renewal of the world and the salvation of the human race, the healing of the human heart and the reordering of all human relationships. For you will recall the words of the Lord Jesus, how he said, "This cup is the new covenant in my blood. Do this, as often as you drink it, in remembrance of me" (1 Cor. 11:25).

In the cross of Christ, in his life poured out for the making of the new covenant, in his death on our behalf and in our place, a transaction of unimaginable grace and mercy has taken place. Our condition was hopeless, but now it is taken up into

Christ's divine life. Everything is changed for us. There is a new promise written in the blood of Christ. In his saving recapitulation of the human story, we see the future of God's redeemed creation.

And so the next time we are tempted to go along with whatever the corrupt world is doing, we can say to ourselves, "I am a creature of the new covenant. God has written his commandments in my heart. I am not the same person that I was. I have been planted by the stream of living water, and if there is a drought, I will still be fed by the unconquerable purpose of God." Every Christian who lives by this promise is a sign planted by God in this world that groans for its redemption.

> Blessed is the man [woman] ... whose trust is the Lord. He [she] is like a tree planted by water, that sends out its roots by the stream, and does not fear when heat comes, for its leaves remain green, and is not anxious in the year of drought, for it does not cease to bear fruit.

PRAYER

O God, the strength of all who put their trust in thee: Mercifully accept our prayers; and because through the weakness of our mortal nature, we can do no good thing without thee, give us the help of thy grace, that in keeping thy commandments we may please thee both in will and deed; through Jesus Christ our Lord, who liveth and reigneth with thee and the Holy Spirit, one God, for ever and ever. *Amen.*

Romans 1:18–3:31

There is no distinction ... all have sinned and fall short of the glory of God.

—ROMANS 3:22–23

In the first three chapters of Romans, Paul, in an elaborate argument, addresses the Christians in Rome on the subject of ungodliness and wickedness (1:18). First, using the pronoun "they," Paul describes the condition of sinful humankind (1:25, 29–32). Up to this point, Paul's readers will have been nodding their heads in agreement. Yes indeed, those people over there are intolerant, narrow-minded, vindictive, bad-mannered, lazy, dishonest, pushy, hypocritical, and unchristian. We can certainly understand that God would be very displeased with *them*.

But Paul turns the argument around. Instead of saying "they," he suddenly starts saying "you." Now he is addressing the moral people, the religious people (2:1–3). Just because God has been good to you, Paul suggests, do you believe yourself to be out of the reach of his wrath? On the contrary,

> In passing judgment upon another, you condemn yourself.... You are storing up wrath for yourself on the day of wrath when God's righteous judgment will be revealed. (2:1, 5)

Paul's argument is based on a distinction between Jews and gentiles. The gentiles are the foreigners, the strangers, the people who are "not our kind." The Jews are the in-group, the religious aristocracy. First he shows that gentiles stand under the judgment of God because of their godlessness; then he turns to the Jewish Christians, who are proud of their special standing with God, and demonstrates that they, too, are deserving of God's wrath. In condemning others, they have presumed to set themselves on a level above condemnation—this is the true meaning of Paul's saying, "In passing judgment upon another, you condemn yourself." He concludes his argument in this way:

> All human beings, both Jews and Gentiles, are under the power of sin.... None is righteous, no, not one. (3:9–10)

> There is no distinction.... All have sinned and fall short of the glory of God. (3:22–23)

To understand what this is all about, we have to empty our minds of all the ideas that we were raised with concerning sin. Almost all of us were brought up to believe that sin has to do with specific forbidden acts. But that is not what the Bible means by sin at all. There is a big difference between sins (plural) and Sin (singular).

Sins (with an *s*) are individual transgressions—fibs, shoplifting, speeding, cheating the government, things like that. We've all managed to convince ourselves that these things aren't too bad, that everybody has a few secret sins, and so what? Over against this we have the predominant biblical view that Sin is a condition. It is a disease, an infection, that the whole human race has got.

All this is summed up in what is often referred to as the doctrine of original sin. Reinhold Niebuhr has spoken of "the good news of original sin," and that's profoundly true. That's why Paul begins his letter with seventeen verses of good news before he gets to the bad. It is a great mistake, however, to skip the bad news altogether, as most people do in the churches today. God's grace is absolutely *free*, but it is not *cheap*.[14] To be a Christian is primarily to know God's grace, but it is also to know the enormity of human resistance to that grace and the price that God paid to overcome that resistance.

We need to know the facts of our condition, and the facts as Paul outlines them are these:

• "All human beings are under the power of Sin" (3:9).
• God hates sin: "the wrath of God is revealed from heaven against all ungodliness and wickedness of men" (1:18).

Let us be quite clear about what Sin is. Let us not trivialize it or domesticate it. Sin is not a matter of a few sins here and a few sins there. Sin is the basic condition of man, the condition of rebellion against God. Sin is a condition we are all heir to; it is a demonic Power that enslaves us and binds us and prevents us from being either free or good. We are responsible before God for Sin, and yet we are unable to liberate ourselves from its grip. We are in a desperate situation, deserving of God's wrath and marked out for his judgment, each of us individually and all of us collectively.

We are not going to turn the corner today. It is good for us to sit with Paul's words for a while: "There is no distinction.... All have sinned.... The wrath of God is revealed from heaven against all ungodliness and wickedness of men." It is good for us to meditate on the knowledge of the reality of sin and the reality of God's anger against Sin. It is good for us to know that God's forgiveness is not simply automatic, as though we could take it for granted.

Let us not evade. Let us not flinch from the truth about ourselves. Let us submit to the word of the apostle, as sisters and brothers in the same sinking lifeboat: "There is no distinction.... All have sinned.... There is none righteous, no, not one." There is not one of us that is not guilty—guilty of hurting our spouses and children and friends, guilty of self-indulgence and self-hatred, guilty of jealousy and dishonesty and laziness and selfishness, guilty of seeking power for ourselves at someone else's expense, guilty of not behaving like Christians, guilty of not caring, guilty of worshiping gods other than the one true God. And the point here is to summon every one of us to realize and to confess that the words of Saint Paul, "All have sinned," refer to us personally, and not to somebody else. It is one of the great works of the Holy Spirit to convict us of sin. Thus we know that the conviction itself is a working of the grace of God.

Let us therefore finish with the words of Thomas Cranmer's great Confession for Morning and Evening Prayer.

PRAYER

Almighty and most merciful Father, we have erred and strayed from thy ways like lost sheep. We have followed too much the devices and desires of our own hearts. We have offended against thy holy laws. We have left undone those things which we ought to have done, and we have done those things which we ought not to have done; and there is no health in us. But thou, O Lord, have mercy upon us, miserable offenders. Spare thou those who confess their faults. Restore those who are penitent; according to thy promises declared unto mankind in Christ Jesus our Lord. And grant, O most merciful Father, for his sake, that we may hereafter live a godly, righteous and sober life, to the glory of thy holy Name. Amen.

Romans 11:25–36

God has consigned all men to disobedience, that he may have mercy upon all.

—ROMANS 11:32

I t is often said nowadays that the church has to give up using words like "redemption," "salvation," and "justification" because people don't know what they mean. My own experience preaching would suggest that that is not true. In any case, the Bible remains wise from age to age; those words are used repeatedly throughout the Scriptures, but in addition, there are hundreds, if not thousands, of stories and illustrations from ordinary life. That, as every literary critic knows, is the secret of the Bible's hold on the imagination of humanity: the stories that illustrate the meaning of the words.

The story of the Bible is the story of God coming to the rescue. God declares to Moses from the burning bush that he has seen the suffering of his people. "I have seen the oppression of my people who are in Egypt, and I have heard their cry because of their taskmasters, for I know their sorrows. So I have come down to deliver them out of the hand of the Egyptians" (Exod. 3:7–8). The Passover and the exodus are the shaping events of Hebrew history, and for Jews and Christians alike they are the central images of God's activity, so much so that the earliest Christians immediately understood the crucifixion and resurrection as the new Passover and exodus, the climax of the drama of deliverance. The Christian story is a story of discovering that we are safe, that we are home, that God has smiled on us. The Good Shepherd has come down and has gathered his lost sheep into his fold; in the words of the hymn, "Perverse and foolish oft I strayed / but yet in love he sought me, / And on his shoulder gently laid, / and home, rejoicing, brought me."[15]

Not everybody knows that they are in need of rescue. A lot of people are unable or unwilling to admit that they are in trouble. There are two kinds of trouble: the kind that is imposed from the outside, and the kind that comes from within. Contrary to popular opinion in some circles, admission of fault is not a weakness; it is a strength. It is very difficult to forgive a person who does not think she needs any forgiveness. It is very hard to go forward with any sort of relationship when there is no recognition of error and no repentance. Without repentance, we cannot understand the truth of our situation. Without a clear-sighted understanding of our need for God's redemption, we will be forever ignorant of the greatness of what the living God has done for us.

The biblical story of salvation tells us that God has smiled down on us. It has already happened. It has already been accomplished. We are safe; we are home. Jesus has done it all for us already. I have often referred to the Swiss legend beloved by Karl Barth about the man who, lost on horseback in the middle of the night, crossed the frozen Lake Constance without realizing what he was doing. When he reached safety on the other side and was told of the terrible fate he had just narrowly escaped, his knees buckled under him in terror and relief. This is the situation we are in. We have already arrived on the other side, because God has declared his favor and goodness toward us. If we do not recognize the seriousness of the predicament we were in, however, then we will never know the greatness of the rescue that has been accomplished for us by our Lord.

The text today is the end of Romans 11, the theological and

also the emotional center of this epistle. Some, and I am one of them, think it is the radical heart of the whole Bible. I call your attention to chapter 11, verse 32: "God has consigned all men to disobedience, that he may have mercy upon all." This is the human story. We have all suffered the effects of sin and disobedience. Not only as individuals but also as communities, cities, groups, and nations, we are poisoned with greed, jealousy, violence, discord, strife, self-seeking of every kind. Jeremiah the prophet found himself lowered into a pit with mire at the bottom, as we read in chapter 38, but his personal plight was not as dreadful to him as the impending judgment he saw hanging over Israel: "Since my people are crushed, I am crushed; I mourn, and horror grips me. Is there no balm in Gilead? Is there no physician there? Why then is there no healing for the wound of my people?" (Jer. 8:21-22).

When Jeremiah spoke those words, he had every reason to believe that the answer was *no, there was no balm* in Gilead. If we don't understand that there really might not have been any, we will never understand the magnitude of God's saving work. The Swiss horseman would never have known what he had escaped if no one had explained it to him.

"God has consigned all men to disobedience, that he may have mercy upon all." As surely as you and I are sunk in a pit of selfishness, idolatry, and godlessness, so surely has the Lord reached down to us "with a mighty hand and an outstretched arm," as the Old Testament says. As surely as we are deserving of God's wrath and condemnation, so surely has his own Son come to take our place in the pit, to rescue us. As Paul writes in Romans 5, "Since we have now been justified by [Christ's] blood, how much more shall we be saved from God's wrath by him! For if, when we were God's enemies, we were reconciled to him through the death of his Son, how much more, having been reconciled, shall we be saved through his life! Not only is this so, but we also *rejoice* in God through our Lord Jesus Christ" (Rom. 5:9-11).

We are all sinners. We are a very long way from true righteousness. But the gospel can give us a kind of joy that comes with the knowledge of deliverance—deliverance from fear now, and the promise of deliverance from condemnation in God's final reckoning. There is an incomparable freedom and lightness in knowing that God knows the worst about us and has nevertheless found the way to rectify all that is wrong. "Rejoice! Again I say, rejoice!"

PRAYER

Most loving Father, who willest us to give thanks for all things, to dread nothing but the loss of thee, and to cast all our care on thee who carest for us: Preserve us from faithless fears and worldly anxieties, and grant that no clouds of this mortal life may hide from us the light of that love which is immortal, and which thou hast manifested to us in thy Son Jesus Christ our Lord; who liveth and reigneth with thee, in the unity of the Holy Spirit, one God, now and for ever. Amen.

1 Corinthians 13; Luke 9:28–36

Love bears all things, believes all things, hopes all things, endures all things. Love never ends.

—1 CORINTHIANS 13:7-8

I remember a very funny little article that appeared in the *New York Times* Styles section one year about the fact that Valentine's Day fell on the Saturday of a three-day holiday weekend. How long, the writer wondered, was the romantic mood expected to continue? After the roses and the chocolates and the candlelight dinner on Saturday night, then what to do for an encore on Sunday? Must you do it all over again? The writer continued, "What about Monday? Can you get out of there by then? What is this anyway—some sort of love Olympics?"[16]

The famous Corinthian chapter on love is not really about the kind of romantic love that this funny article gently mocks, though it is so often read at weddings; it really describes Jesus. He is the supreme model of mature love, today and forever. Jesus "is patient and kind"; Jesus "is not jealous or boastful"; Jesus "is not arrogant or rude." The capacity to postpone gratification lies at the very heart of mature love: Jesus "does not insist on his own way." The love of Jesus "never ends." It's a good bet that most wedding guests hearing 1 Corinthians 13 understand it sentimentally, not being aware that the passage is really about the love of Christ as it takes shape in the Christian community.

This Sunday is a major turning point in the church's year. Today, the transfigured Christ turns his blazing face toward disfigurement and certain death in Jerusalem at the hands of his enemies. This week, the church turns away from the light of Epiphany into the shadows of Lent. Look again at Saint Luke's account of the story that is read on this day: "Now about eight days after these sayings, Jesus took with him Peter and John and James, and went up on the mountain to pray. And as he was praying, the appearance of his countenance was altered, and his raiment became dazzling white. And behold, two men talked with him, Moses and Elijah, who appeared in glory and spoke of his departure, which he was to accomplish at Jerusalem."

This event—called the transfiguration—is the most unambiguous revelation of Jesus as Messiah prior to the resurrection. As Peter, James, and John watch the dazzling scene, the voice of God himself declares Jesus to be his Son. The appearance of Moses and Elijah ratifies the designation of Jesus as the Chosen One of Israel, the fulfillment of the Law (Moses) and the Prophets (Elijah). This is the original "mountaintop experience." The text says our old friend Peter, always the one to speak first and later to regret it, says: "Let us make three booths, one for you and one for Moses and one for Elijah," but didn't know what he was saying.

It is part of our fallen human nature to want to build booths and ski lodges and resort hotels on top of mountains. We don't want to come down from the high. We want the love Olympics to go on indefinitely. Jesus, however, is the one truly new person. He knows he cannot stay on the summit soaking up the view. He and Moses and Elijah speak together, but not of peak experiences. They speak of "his departure, which he was to accomplish at Jerusalem."

"And a cloud came and overshadowed them; and [the disciples] were afraid." Peter and James and John saw two things that day on the mountain. They saw Jesus with the veil lifted to reveal his glory; and then they saw the clouds coming.

For, you see, love cannot stay on the mountaintop. It must come down. Love must go where it is most needed in the valley of the shadow of death. The passage from 1 Corinthians is read today because it is about Jesus as he sets forth to be crucified.

Love *comes down.* "Love bears all things, believes all things, hopes all things, endures all things." Love is grateful for the experience on the mountaintop but knows that it cannot stay there. Love persists when the glory has faded, when the romance has fled, when the curtain has been dropped on the stage set. Love never gives up. The King James Version is stronger in some ways; Love "suffereth long and is kind; love vaunteth not itself; is not puffed up, doth not behave itself unseemly, is not easily provoked...love never faileth." Love does not even require reciprocity; love goes to Jerusalem, where the enemy lies in wait.

A book by Taylor Branch, *Pillar of Fire,* tells part of the story of the civil rights movement. It comes to a climax with Martin Luther King Jr. traveling to Oslo as the guest of the king of Sweden to receive the Nobel Peace Prize. As the undisputed leader of a movement that had captured the imagination of people around the globe, he had access to the crowned heads of Europe and the inner circles of power in Washington. Surely he could not be faulted if he had retired from the barricades, directing future operations from the rear. Here are two sentences from the final paragraph of Taylor Branch's book: "Martin Luther King confronted furies ahead ... [his] inner course was *fixed downward,* toward the sanitation workers of Memphis."[17] In Memphis, there was a bullet waiting.

Love bears all things, endures all things. On this day, Jesus turns his back on his glory and begins his descent into the valley. He comes down from the mountain; he comes down from the throne of the majesty on high; he comes down from the infinite spaces of uncreated light and prepares to enter the darkness of human suffering and human pain. God is not looking down with detachment from a great distance. God did not remain majestically aloof somewhere over the rainbow. God is not a distant observer of our struggles. As Jesus of Nazareth sets his face toward Jerusalem, he is about to become in his own person the embrace of God for all the misery of all the world.

And so wherever one human being reaches out for another in the midst of suffering, wherever a person in power stoops down to help, wherever the mighty bend to the lowly, there is the Lord. Whenever you do this, you are becoming Jesus's disciple. And whoever you are and whatever your pain, this very day in the power of his Word spoken, he reaches out, he comes down, to seek *you*, to find *you*, to embrace *you*. The love Olympics have gone to Jerusalem.

PRAYER

O God, who before the passion of thy only-begotten Son didst reveal his glory upon the holy mount: Grant unto us that we, beholding by faith the light of his countenance, may be strengthened to bear our cross, and be changed into his likeness from glory to glory; through Jesus Christ our Lord, who liveth and reigneth with thee and the Holy Spirit, one God, for ever and ever. *Amen.*

LENT
AND
HOLY WEEK

Psalm 51

> Against thee, thee only, I have sinned,
>   and done that which is evil in thy sight.

—PSALM 51:4

Psalm 51, the Ash Wednesday psalm, is the acknowledged masterpiece of biblical self-knowledge. "I have been wicked from my birth, a sinner from my mother's womb." No human being has ever looked at himself more unflinchingly than the author of this incomparable penitential psalm. "I know my transgressions, and my sin is ever before me." On Ash Wednesday we acknowledge that God has a case against us, and we throw ourselves on his mercy.

There is a strange statement in verse 4 of Psalm 51: "Against you [God] only have I sinned and done what is evil in your sight." Why does he say that he has sinned only against God? Sin hurts everybody—it hurts those who are victimized, exploited, used, damaged, scorned, and neglected as a result of pride, greed, anger, lust, envy, and self-will. Why does the psalmist say he has sinned against God only?

The reason for this is of central importance. Sin, at bottom, is not an *ethical* concept at all. It is a *theological* concept. Sin is only understood to be sin when God is understood to be God. The recognition of sin comes as the psalmist is confronted in prayer with the reality of God, the power of God, the holiness of God, who has the absolute right to make demands and render judgments. "You are justified when you speak." We need to learn this; we are so accustomed to the kind of reasoning that says, "But I'm not hurting anybody," "Nobody will know," "Everybody else is doing it," "It isn't anybody's business." But in the last analysis, the Bible reveals, every sinful action, every sinful thought, is directed against God. Our concept of sin, like our concept of God, is too small until we learn to say with the psalmist, "Against you [God] only have I sinned and done what is evil in your sight."

The genius of Psalm 51, and the source of its ageless significance, is this: in its impassioned petitions, the psalmist demonstrated that *he has learned to see sin as God sees it*.[18] When we see that sin is an offense against the author of all goodness, then it floods in upon us that the goodness of the Lord is precisely the place where all our sin is lifted up and done away with. The recognition of sin is our *response to* God's holiness and mercy. On Ash Wednesday, as we look into the depths, not only of our own sin but that of the whole human race, even as we consciously acknowledge the seriousness of our predicament before God, *at that same moment* we recognize God as the one who extends his mercy to us even in the midst of our condition. As Paul wrote: "While we were *still sinners*, Christ died for us" (Rom. 5:8).

Look at the psalm again. It begins,

> Have mercy on me, O God, according to your
>   lovingkindness:
>   in your great compassion blot out my offenses.

This is a prayer of a person who knows there is hope, who knows there is mercy, who knows that God is full of compassion. The knowledge of grace has preceded the confession of sin. The person who confesses sin in this free way, holding nothing back, making no excuses, blaming no one but himself, is the person who knows that God is truly able to do away with sin and make a completely new person out of the sinner. The author of Psalm 51 knows this. He prays, "Create in me a clean heart, O God, and renew a right spirit within me."

So great is his confidence in God that he is able to refer to himself as a miserable offender and, *at the same time*, to say "make me hear of joy and gladness." The combination of uttermost penitence and unconquerable confidence lies at the very heart of the knowledge of who we are before God and what he intends for us.

This is Ash Wednesday. This is the day in the year set apart for the most searching self-inventory before God, the most honest assessment of our sinful nature that we can possibly offer him. Our temptation will be, as always, to try to squirm off the hook in some way. But, you see, all these evasions fall pitifully short of the reality and power and holiness of the living God. God has shown us a great thing. We do not need to surround ourselves with defenses and barricades. We do not need to lie to ourselves and others. We do not need to live out an exhausting, lifelong charade of pretense lest someone discover that we are not what we appear to be. In the Christian community, we can let ourselves be seen as the sinners we really are.

There is Another who has taken the sentence upon himself, and in so doing, has nullified it. Jesus, the Son of God, has voluntarily taken our place. He himself hung naked on the cross, bearing in his own body the storm of the wrath of God against sin. As Saint Paul writes, "God made [Jesus] to be sin who knew no sin, that in him we might become the righteousness of God" (2 Cor. 5:21).

PRAYER

Almighty and everlasting God, who hatest nothing that thou hast made and dost forgive the sins of all those who are penitent: Create and make in us new and contrite hearts, that we,

worthily lamenting our sins and acknowledging our wretchedness, may obtain of thee, the God of all mercy, perfect remission and forgiveness; through Jesus Christ our Lord, who
liveth and reigneth with thee and the Holy Spirit, one God, for
ever and ever. *Amen.*

Psalm 19

Who can discern his errors?
Clear thou me from my hidden faults.

—PSALM 19:12

I n late 1944, while the Allies were rapidly advancing across
Europe after the success of the Normandy invasion, J. R. R.
Tolkien, the author of *Lord of the Rings*, wrote a letter to his son
Christopher, who was serving in the RAF (the British Royal Air
Force). Tolkien himself, the father, had fought the Germans in
World War I; he was in the infamous trenches of the Battle of
the Somme. Obviously this father and son were not pacifists.
It is therefore all the more notable that Tolkien wrote to his
son that he was very disturbed by the way the British press
was relentlessly depicting all Germans as irremediably evil.
He quoted from one of the local English newspapers, whose
editor was seriously advocating "systematic extermination" of
the entire German nation because "they are rattlesnakes and
don't know the difference between good and evil." Tolkien
continued:

> *What of the writer?* The Germans have just as much right to
> declare ... the Jews exterminable vermin, subhuman, as we
> have to select the Germans: in other words, no right, what-
> ever they've done.[19]

Whenever a person takes to himself (or herself) the defining of another person or group as evil, he is in more danger than he knows. It is in the very nature of the human being to judge other people and groups as evil. We can then give ourselves permission to treat those others as less than fully human, to ostracize them or persecute them and eventually to destroy them. And once we have begun that game, it takes on a life of its own and it begins to dominate us without our even noticing.

The enemy lines are hard to find. The axis of evil lies here, there, and everywhere. Aleksandr Solzhenitsyn wrote these words from the Soviet gulag:

> Gradually it was disclosed to me that the line separating good and evil passes not through states, nor between classes, nor between political parties either—but right through every human heart.... This line shifts. Inside us, it oscillates with the years. And even within hearts overwhelmed by evil, one small bridgehead of good is retained. And even in the best of all hearts there remains ... an uprooted small corner of evil.[20]

The season of Lent reminds the Christian community that the line runs through you and the line runs through me. It reminds us to beware of drawing lines between ourselves on the good side and others on the bad side. In the words of Psalm 51, "I know my transgressions, and my sin is ever before me." In the words of our psalm for today, "Who can tell how often he offends? Cleanse thou me from my secret faults" (Ps. 19:12).

When we cannot hear such things about ourselves without bristling and becoming defensive, we are in trouble. When we are unable to utter a sincere apology and ask for forgiveness, our primary relationships are in trouble. When a nation treats dissent as unpatriotic, the whole world is in trouble. Repentance, the Lenten theme, is necessary for human well-being. Our leaders in former times seemed to know this. Our two greatest presidents, George Washington and Abraham Lincoln, both called the nation to repentance. It is hard to imagine any president of either political party doing that today.

Frederica Mathewes-Green gave a new definition in an article I read. "Repentance is not blubbering and self-loathing. Repentance is insight."[21]

Repentance is insight. Repentance is not groveling. Moreover, repentance is quite a different thing from saying "I'm sorry if anyone was offended" a dozen times. Repentance involves trying to understand *why* people were offended, *why* people were hurt, *why* people would like to hear a true and sincere apology, and why we ourselves have been offenders. "Who can tell how often he offends? Cleanse thou me from my secret faults."

All of us share in the human condition; that is the secret of this season of Lent. All of us have dark impulses that could have become murderous had we been brought up in brutal circumstances or been catechized by a vengeful father full of hate. Let me be clear: action has to be taken against evil deeds. But the Christian will beware lest more evil deeds begin to erupt *from within* as well as from without.

It is God's plan to have mercy upon us. He "has consigned all human beings to disobedience, that he may have mercy upon all" (Rom. 11:32). The First Epistle of Peter puts it another way: "Jesus Christ also died for sins once for all, the righteous for the unrighteous, that he might bring us to God" (1 Pet. 3:18). The righteous died for the unrighteous: that is to say, he, the only truly righteous one, died for the unrighteous. And again Paul: "While we were still helpless, Christ died for the ungodly" (Rom. 5:6).

A great mistake we could make today is to think of ourselves in the wrong category. The Lord Jesus did not die for the righteous. He did not die for the godly. He did not die for the exceptional so that we, the saved, could delight in our own superiority and gloat over others. The Bible teaches us to see ourselves as God sees us. Suppose you and I were at the mercy of what our enemies think of us. Thanks be to God, the ultimate destiny of human beings is not to be determined by enemies. We live and die at the mercy of God, "to whom all hearts are open, all desires known, and from whom no secrets are hid." "Cleanse thou me from my secret faults, O God."

God sees you as you really are, and he loves you. God sees those parts of you that you hide even from yourself, and he loves you. God sees us all dividing up the world into good and evil, but he, the only one entitled to divide the evil from the good, the one who could have remained enthroned above our struggles, out of his love came into the world to be "numbered among the transgressors" (Isa. 53:12). Through his Son Jesus Christ he has entered into our condition, bowing his head under the onslaught of human vengefulness, indifference, cruelty, and hate in order to show mercy to us all, *especially to the perpetrators.*

He died the death of an outcast; he died the death of a condemned man; he died the death of one who had been declared an enemy of all the righteous of the state and of the church. With the last breath of his body and the last drop of his blood, he has wrought the salvation of his enemies: that is to say, the salvation of each and every one of us.

PRAYER

Almighty God . . . make speed to help thy servants who are assaulted by manifold temptations; and, as thou knowest their several infirmities, let each one find thee mighty to save; through Jesus Christ thy Son our Lord, who liveth and reigneth with thee and the Holy Spirit, one God, now and for ever. Amen.

John 4:1–42; Romans 5:6–8

> While we were still weak, at the right time Christ died for the ungodly.... God shows his love for us in that while we were yet sinners Christ died for us.
>
> —ROMANS 5:6, 8

When my children were little I drove a lot of car pools. It was always very illuminating because the children would forget that I was there and would talk about other children. "Matthew is a jerk." "Mary's clothes are stupid." It was a perfect demonstration of original sin, an ailment that afflicts every human being on this earth. We all play this game. We can always find someone worse that we feel superior to. We all divide up people into classes and groups, in order to believe that we are in the best group and somebody else is in the worst. Insecure as we are, this is a universal phenomenon. We're not like them; we would hate to be them.

When Jesus was on this earth, he did not obey this universal human rule of behavior. Instead, he acted in a way that got him into trouble everywhere he went. What did Jesus do that made everybody, and especially the religious people, so mad? Let's take a look at a story from the Gospel of John.

Jesus went into a village of Samaria. Now you need to know that Samaria was not a good neighborhood. In Jesus's time, Judea was good, Galilee was not so good, and Samaria was, as we say, the pits. Jews like Jesus did not go to Samaria if they could help it. Parents wouldn't want their children to go to Samaritan schools.

Jesus, however, deliberately went into this bad neighborhood. According to the story in John's Gospel, he was tired from his long walk, so he sat down by the village well. Jesus got tired, just as we do. He understands what it is like to be human. He isn't above us, looking down on us and saying, "John is a loser. Sally is a failure. Michael is a weakling." He came among us in our weaknesses and failures and losses.

Nobody in Jesus's time had running water except the Roman aristocracy. Every town in those days had a well, and you had to go to the well to get your water. When Jesus arrived, there was nobody there, because it was the middle of the day, hot and dusty. The women did not come for their water until the cool of the early evening, when they could visit a little with each other and exchange news before getting back to the kitchen. But then: a woman, all alone, with her big water jug balanced on her shoulder. Why is she coming in the middle of the day? We soon find out. Jesus looks up at this Samaritan woman and says, "Give me a drink."

Jesus lowered himself another notch here. He couldn't even draw his own water, because he had no container to put it in. He was dependent on the woman to help him. This was not the way a dignified Jewish man was supposed to act. Jesus, however, was not ashamed to place himself in the company of those who are needy.

Now, the story turns at this point. We learn that this woman is not only a Samaritan, not only a woman. She is an outcast in a community of outcasts. Even among Samaritans, this woman is beyond the pale.

Jesus said to the Samaritan woman, Go, bring your husband to the well. The woman said, I have no husband. Jesus replied, "You are right in saying, 'I have no husband,' for you have had five husbands, and he whom you now have is not your husband; this you said truly." That is the reason the woman was coming to the well in the middle of the day; she did not want to face the other women of the town. She had had too many men in her life. She was not a good wife and mother like the other women. They looked down on her. "We're not like her," they would say. "We would hate to be her."

We learn from the story that even the woman herself was amazed by Jesus's behavior: she said to him, "How is it that you, a Jew, ask a drink of me, a woman of Samaria? For Jews have no dealings with Samaritans." One of the most important things to remember about Jesus is that he made a special point of reaching out to the people that no one else wanted to be with. Jesus made a most wonderful promise to the Samaritan woman in the story: "Whoever drinks of the water that I shall give him will never thirst; the water that I shall give will become in him a spring of water welling up to eternal life." The woman was so thrilled that she left her water jar behind at the well and rushed off to tell everyone that she could find—and Saint John tells us that, as a result, "Many Samaritans from that place believed in [Jesus] because of the woman's testimony." Jesus caused that outcast woman to become a missionary, an evangelist. In the event of meeting Jesus, the unholy Samaritan woman became the equal of any upstanding Jewish man.

That is what Jesus does. He reaches out especially to those who are outcast and downtrodden, and he transforms them. He gives them water for eternal life. The water that Jesus gives is his own self, his own divine life. In receiving Jesus, we become new people. We begin a new journey. We won't want to set ourselves up against others. We won't want to divide up the world into good neighborhoods and bad neighborhoods. We will understand that even those who live in nice neighborhoods don't have clean hands and a pure heart.

So the miracle of today's story is that the Lord's wonderful message today is for every one of us. Saint Paul makes it clear in the second reading for today:

While we were still helpless, Christ died for the ungodly....
God shows his love for us in that while we were still sinners
Christ died for us. (Rom. 5:6, 8)

He didn't wait until we had clean hands and a pure heart. He
didn't say, "God helps those who help themselves." While we
were still *helpless*, Jesus died for *unrighteous* people, *immoral*
people, *ungodly* people. These two verses from Romans are the
very heart of the Bible: *Christ died for the ungodly*. For you see, in
the Lord's sight, all of us are ungodly Samaritans, but *while we
were still sinners Christ died for us*.

Draw near today with renewed faith as our living Lord
speaks to us all in the words he spoke to that outcast Samaritan
woman: "Whoever drinks of the water that I shall give him will
never thirst; the water that I shall give him will become in him
a spring of water welling up to eternal life."

PRAYER

O God, whose glory it is always to have mercy: Be gracious to
all who have gone astray from thy ways, and bring them again
with penitent hearts and steadfast faith to embrace and hold
fast the unchangeable truth of thy Word, Jesus Christ thy Son;
who with thee and the Holy Spirit liveth and reigneth, one
God, for ever and ever. Amen.

Mark 10:45

"The Son of man also came not to be served but to serve, and to give his life as a ransom for many."

—MARK 10:45

This word "ransom." Think about it for a moment. What is the purpose of a ransom? Clearly it is for deliverance. The basic idea is this:

1. A person or group has come under the control of another power.
2. The person or group has lost its freedom to act.
3. The person or group finds its own strength completely inadequate.
4. *Therefore*: Freedom can be gained only through the intervention of an outside power.

The most obvious modern analogy is hostages locked in a building. They can't free themselves. An antiterrorist squad has to come in from outside. Think of occupied Europe held hostage under the Nazis. There were valiant resistance movements here and there, but as long as they operated from within the Nazi realm, there was no real hope. There had to be an *invasion*, a landing that would liberate them from the occupying forces. C. S. Lewis's Narnia stories are based on the same premise. The inhabitants of Narnia are in thrall to the wicked queen of Narnia and cannot escape her power; they must wait for the mighty lion, Aslan, to land. Once the invasion has begun, they know they will be freed.

The New Testament sees the situation very much in these terms. The creation is not free; nature and human beings alike are not free; we are all under the sway of occupying Powers: Sin, Evil, Death. Only an invasion by the Creator himself can save it. In the incarnation of the Son of God, the invasion has begun; in the crucifixion the beachheads are secured; in the resurrection we see the firstfruits of the final liberation.

There were important early theologians who thought Jesus's death was a ransom paid to the devil. Most ordinary Christians to this day, however, have probably understood the "ransom saying" for what it is: a figure of speech. Vincent Taylor called it a "luminous hint."[22] The emphasis in the idea of a ransom is *deliverance by purchase.*[23] The First Epistle of Peter clarifies it: "You know that you were ransomed from the futile ways inherited from your fathers, not with perishable things such as silver or gold, but with the precious blood of Christ, like that of a lamb without blemish or spot" (1 Pet. 1:18–19). This passage contains the idea of original sin ("futile ways"), holding us in bondage as it did our parents and grandparents and so on back as far as we can trace the human species. Saint Paul, especially, sees humanity in bondage to hostile Powers and depicts the cross as the moment of deliverance. Twice in close succession, as though to emphasize it, he writes to the Corinthians: "You were bought with a price" (1 Cor. 6:20; 7:23). Again, the idea of a ransom or price is a metaphor, conveying the idea that the price to be paid is of equivalent value to that which is redeemed.

Here is the key to our participation in the story. We were held hostage to Sin and Death. These two Powers rose up with all their might, wielding their weapons so effectively that all the best people fell in line to acquiesce in the execution of the Son of God. On Good Friday he became two things at once: the one-man antiterrorist team and the hostage who steps forward and volunteers to be killed. He is both at the same time.

If you say this doesn't make any earthly sense, you are right. We are stretching for words here. The mysterious ransom saying of Jesus cannot be forced into rational categories. What it tells us is this: God is *personally involving himself* in the rescue of his enslaved children, at the highest level of sacrifice the world has ever seen. It is not just that he has come to set us free. It is more than that. He has in some hitherto unimaginable way actually substituted himself for us, as though our blighted little lives were actually worth this gift of infinite value, this outpouring of the divine life of God, this undergoing of ultimate humiliation, this entrance into hell—for us. Only by looking at the cross of Christ do we learn the magnitude of the forces that held us in bondage. We escaped; he was immolated. The size of the "ransom" is equivalent to the size of our enslavement. That is the payment of equivalent value. That is what we are worth to him.

And so, you see, the price for our complicity in his crucifixion has already been paid. The universal human condition is one of bondage under the reign of Death; but in his own death and resurrection the Lord has overturned that reign. He has established himself forever over the dark Powers. He can never be overthrown. "He reflects the glory of God and bears the very stamp of his nature, upholding the universe by his word of power. When he had made purification for sins, he sat down at the right hand of the Majesty on high" (Heb. 1:3).

"Aslan has landed."[24] Everything is different now. Our struggle continues, but as the English say, we are "in very good heart." D-Day was not the end; in World War II the desperate Battle of the Bulge still remained to be fought, but when you know the enemy is on the run, you fight with a defiant confidence. Winston Churchill said to the British people in 1942, "This is not the end. It is not even the beginning of the end. But it is, perhaps, the end of the beginning." Expanding his words, we may rightly say that the crucifixion and resurrection of Jesus Christ are truly the beginning of the End, when the kingdom of God will be all in all.

PRAYER

Almighty God, who seest that we have no power of ourselves to help ourselves: Keep us both outwardly in our bodies and inwardly in our souls, that we may be defended from all adversities which may happen to the body, and from all evil thoughts which may assault and hurt the soul; through Jesus Christ our Lord, who liveth and reigneth with thee and the Holy Spirit, one God, for ever and ever. *Amen.*

....

Jeremiah 33:1–3; Romans 4:13–25

"Call to me and I will answer you, and will tell you great and hidden things which you have not known."

—JEREMIAH 33:3

L et's think for a moment about hope and hopelessness. In the crucial fourth chapter of the letter to the Romans, the apostle Paul retells the story of Abraham and Sarah, whose situation was definitely hopeless from any human point of view. Despite God's promises about Abraham's descendants, decades have passed and there is no heir.

It's customary to say that Abraham's *faith* was what kept him going, but actually, that isn't quite right. We often say that people are saved by faith, or saved by prayer, but faith and prayer are not anchored in anything without the power of the God who gives them. So it's not Abraham's *faith* that counts, but Abraham's *God*. Our God: the God of Abraham, Isaac, and Jacob, the God and Father of our Lord Jesus Christ. Paul identifies God this way: "the God in whom [Abraham] believed, who gives life to the dead and calls into existence the things that do not exist. In hope [Abraham] believed against hope" (Rom. 4:17–18).

This is one of the greatest texts in all of the Bible, yet many do not know it. Let's hold it in our minds as we think about the nature of God in hopeless situations. Abraham's God, our God, is the one "who gives life to the dead and calls into existence the things that do not exist." This is not the language we use about God as a general rule. We speak of God as loving, forgiving, embracing, inclusive, and so forth, but that doesn't convey the unique generative power of a God who can call things into existence when they do not even exist.

Jeremiah lived a life that was hopeless by any human standard. Jeremiah's entire existence was given over to his vocation of warning the people of Judah to repent of their ways and return to God before it was too late, but—this is the terrible part—he knew they wouldn't do it. He knew that his prophecies wouldn't be taken to heart. He knew that the Babylonians were going to come and sweep everything away. He knew it was hopeless. His life was a misery.

And yet Jeremiah had a hope that was beyond hope. Look at what God said to him:

> The word of the Lord came to Jeremiah ... while he was still shut up in the court of the guard: "Thus says the Lord who made the earth, the Lord who formed it to establish it—the Lord is his name: Call to me and I will answer you, and will tell you great and hidden things which you have not known." (Jer. 33:1–3)

Jeremiah was shut up in the court of the guard. This was one of many times that he suffered abuse and imprisonment. The cataclysm is coming; Jerusalem will fall; the temple will be destroyed and the people taken off to live as exiles in a godless land. Yet the Creator of the universe speaks to Jeremiah, the Lord who formed and established the earth, the God to whom mighty Babylon is but a drop in the bucket (Isa. 40:15). The faith of Jeremiah, like the faith of Abraham, was not worked up out of human religious consciousness. Faith is called into being by the Word of the Lord. God said to Jeremiah: "Call to me and I will answer you, and will tell you great and hidden things which your human imagination cannot produce."

The key that unlocks the hope beyond hope is the knowledge of God. No matter what the various "spiritual" experts tell us in all their various talk shows, best sellers, and expensive retreats, God is not a product of the human religious search. God is the one who was already there before we started searching for him. He was there before human imagination existed—the one who is, and who was, and who is to come (Rev. 1:8). God is the one who will reveal great and hidden things *which we have not known*, things that we cannot devise or create. That is the door of the divine hope.

As we grasp this hope that is beyond hope, we learn to loosen our grip on our own hopes. Our idea of what to hope for is limited by our human horizons. We think we know what we want, what is best, what will make us happy, what we need. Most theologically dangerous of all, we think we know *what God owes us*. All of that has to go. We need a larger sense of the God who reveals great and hidden things that we do not know! Our God is so small!

When we pray, we need a larger view of the God whose thoughts, as the prophet Isaiah said, are not our thoughts, whose ways are not our ways (55:8). At the end of our services, Episcopalians sometimes hear the verse from Ephesians: "Glory to God, whose power working in us can do *infinitely more than we can ask or imagine*" (3:20). That's the idea.

As the Day of Resurrection approaches, we need to think about these things. The God of Abraham, the God and Father of Jesus Christ, is doing great and hidden things beyond what we know, beyond what we expect, beyond what we can imagine.

Faith in God is not faith that gives up when God seems to be silent. That would be mere human faith, grounded in human hopes and expectations—expectations that God will answer our prayers in exactly the way we want.

On the final day of resurrection, the Lord will gather in the harvest of all those who have hoped in him. But *not only those* who have hoped in him at the level of an Abraham. Do you know someone who feels hopeless? Are you wondering about someone who has no faith? Is there someone dead whose presence you desperately miss? The God who is powerful to call into existence the things that do not exist is also powerful to create hope where there is no hope, faith where there is no faith, and life where there is no breath. The hope that is beyond hope is the hope that refuses to let go even when the cold clasp of death seems to be the last word, for this is the eternal God who raises the dead. "The Lord is his name."

PRAYER

Gracious Father, whose blessed Son Jesus Christ came down from heaven to be the true bread which giveth life to the world: Evermore give us this bread, that he may live in us, and we in him; who liveth and reigneth with thee and the Holy Spirit, one God, now and for ever. Amen.

Romans 3:9–25

> For there is no distinction; since all have sinned and fall short of the glory of God, [we] are justified by his grace as a gift, through the redemption which is in Christ Jesus, whom God put forward as an expiation by his blood, to be received by faith.

—ROMANS 3:22B–25A

The letter to the Romans begins with the gospel—a ringing introduction in which Paul sets out his theme, saying, "I am not ashamed of the gospel; it is the power of God for salvation to every one who has faith, to the Jew first and also to the Greek" (Rom. 1:16).

But then, startlingly, Paul shifts into the bad news, a long section on the wrath of God that goes on for two and a half chapters. This section rewards careful study. The cumulative effect of this wrath of God section is quite overwhelming. You think that you are off the hook at first, because Paul is going after people other than you (in this case, the gentile heathen), but then he turns the charges around to indict the good religious people too, the ones who thought God approved of them (in this case, the Jews). And so the section comes to a climax with a resounding summary of his case, pronouncing every single human being unrighteous before God and judged by God's law.

We need always to remember something about the wrath of God. The wrath of God does not mean that God is enraged, or cruel, or wicked. Wrath is not an emotion of God. Wrath is the face of Holiness when it is turned toward Sin.[25] The position of humanity before God is that of gross impurity confronted by perfect holiness. We need to deepen our understanding of the vast distance between ourselves and a righteous God. If we are to take account of righteousness, our standing before God is less than nothing. It takes courage and honesty to see that—the courage and honesty that go along with true faith. By faith we see that "all are under the power of sin" (3:9), and all are condemned by God's law in one way or another.

The purpose of the Lenten season is to give us all an opportunity to mourn our captivity under Sin. Paul's cosmic indictment means that we understand ourselves not just as people who commit a little error here and a minor mistake there. We are implicated in a global network of ungodliness. We are not innocent bystanders to the march of Sin throughout the world.

But now. Whenever you hear the words "but now" in Scripture, lift up your heads! The words "but now" are the signal for the arrival of the gospel. In order to grasp this, remember that Paul has shown that we are all condemned under God's law. Here is the place for the turning point:

> But now the righteousness of God has been manifested apart from law ... the righteousness of God through faith in Jesus Christ for all who believe. For there is no distinction; since all have sinned and fall short of the glory of God, they are justified by his grace as a gift, through the redemption which is in Christ Jesus.

The redemption which is in Christ Jesus. What does it mean to *redeem* something? It means to pay a price to buy it back. That's what God has done. He has paid the ultimate price to buy back his world. Whatever cataclysm occurs, it will be no match for God's divine universal purpose. The unrighteousness of all humanity is no match for the righteousness of God.

Think now about yourself. You may not be thinking about global issues right now. You are thinking about the problem you have with your children, or your elderly parents. You are concerned about some of your relationships. Or you are asking yourself if you are really making it in your job. Maybe you have a problem with drinking, or eating, or bad stuff on the Internet. Maybe your bills are too high and your credit is not what it was. You may wonder if you are just a cog in a machine, or if you can really make a difference. If you are reflective, you sometimes ask yourself what your life adds up to.

The good news of God in Jesus Christ is not just a declaration of innocence for the guilty. That would involve God in a cheat. It would be overlooking evil and denying the horrific suffering of many millions. The letter to the Romans declares a gospel far more comprehensive than that. The righteousness of God, which is really the theme of Romans, does not mean that God sits off in heaven being righteous and expressing anger from time to time because we are not righteous. You get that idea from preachers sometimes, but it isn't the gospel. The righteousness of God means that God calls servants for himself whom he then makes righteous. The righteousness of God means that God has given a new law written on the heart, a law that does not condemn but saves.

The righteousness of God means that God takes action. It means that the Red Sea parts and the sun stands still over Gibeon and the Spirit breathes on the dry bones and the trumpet sounds and the dead are raised. It means that God will call into existence the things that do not exist (Rom. 4:17)—which means that there will be peace where there was war, and love where there was hate, and truth where there were lies, and righteousness where there was only unrighteousness, for God did not come to congratulate the worthy but to save sinners, meaning you and me. And that means that there is nothing in the universe, and especially not the wrath of God, that can condemn us, because in the cross of Christ, God himself—the Father and the Son acting together—has found the way to absorb, neutralize, and satisfy his own wrath, for now "the righteousness of God has been manifested apart from the law."

For there is no distinction; since all have sinned and fall short of the glory of God, [we] are justified by his grace as a gift, through the redemption which is in Christ Jesus, whom God put forward as an expiation by his blood, to be received by faith.

PRAYER

O Almighty God, who alone canst order the unruly wills and affections of sinful men: Grant unto thy people that they may love the thing which thou commandest, and desire that which thou dost promise; that so, among the sundry and manifold changes of the world, our hearts may surely there be fixed where true joys are to be found; through Jesus Christ our Lord, who liveth and reigneth with thee and the Holy Spirit, one God, now and for ever. *Amen.*

LITURGY OF THE PALMS

Luke 19:28–44; 23:1–49

When he drew near and saw the city he wept over it.

—LUKE 19:41

Palm Sunday is a very strange day. Its proper name is the Sunday of the Passion, because the story of Jesus's suffering and death is always read. I remember a teenaged boy, an acolyte in my former church, standing with the cross at the head of the palm procession. He turned to me and said, "I don't understand what I'm supposed to be feeling." He well captured the ambivalence of the day. Crowds are attracted by the festivity and then get hit over the head with the story of the crucifixion. It is not a day for the faint of heart.

Let us take our cue from Saint Luke and the other evangelists, since the center of every Palm Sunday service is the reading of the passion narrative from the Gospel of Matthew, Mark, or Luke. This week more than any other, we come to the center of what they want to communicate to us. We have just read Luke's version of the passion. All four of the Gospels move toward this climax. All four of them give much more attention to the suffering and crucifixion of Jesus than they do to any other part of his life. This is not an accident. From the earliest days of the church, it was understood that Jesus's life gained its significance from his death. The apostles and evangelists wanted their readers to understand the meaning of this death more than they wanted anything else in the world.

Palm Sunday is not a day unto itself. Palm Sunday is the introduction to Holy Week. When Jesus came into Jerusalem riding on that donkey, he was received with something like the sort of acclaim that celebrities receive today. Jesus was mobbed, so to speak. His head, however, was not turned. He seems to have known exactly what was happening to him. In Saint Luke's version of the Palm Sunday story, he tells us that "when he drew near and saw the city he wept over it, saying, 'Would that even today you knew the things that make for peace! But now they are hid from your eyes. For the days shall come upon you, when your enemies will . . . hem you in on every side, and dash you to the ground, you and your children within you, and they will not leave one stone upon another in you; because you did not know the time of your visitation'" (Luke 19:41–44). Here is the purpose of the Palm Sunday liturgy: for the church to know the things that make for her peace, to know the time of her visitation. And strangely enough, it is in precisely the agony of the cross that the church finds her peace.

This is one of only two times in the four Gospels that we are told Jesus wept. Surely this is extraordinary. The Gospel of Luke says he is weeping for the city. What is the city? It is God's holy city, or was supposed to be; but what a long, long history of disobedience and disappointment! How Jerusalem had abandoned her holy calling! For a thousand years God had been preparing her through the prophets to meet her Messiah, her Savior, her Redeemer; now, as the Messiah at last appears, she is going to arrest him on a trumped-up charge, try him in the middle of the night, flog him nearly to death, and execute him the way we execute serial killers and terrorist bombers, though in an infinitely worse manner. Yet Jesus does not weep for himself. He weeps for the city. He weeps for those who will soon shout, "Crucify him!" In other words, he weeps for us.

Did anyone ever weep for you? Did your mother shed tears

because you did something that disappointed her? Did your
father weep for you because you got into trouble? Or did a
daughter weep because her father abused her? Did a son weep
because his mother blamed him for something he never did?
Did you weep for a friend lost on the battlefield or in an air
crash? Did you weep for a child lost in drug culture or for a
grandchild kicked out of school? Did you weep for someone
committing a hideous injustice? All these tears and every tear
that has ever been shed by anyone anywhere are rolled up into
the tears of Jesus. Jesus weeps for us. The Son of God weeps
for you.

Tears are eloquent. Tears speak. Jesus's tears encompass the
entire human tragedy; he weeps for human pain, yes, *but also
for human sin.*

Why is it that we don't like the cross? Why would we just
as soon skip Good Friday and come back to church on Easter
Day when everything will be beautiful? Well, there are a lot of
reasons, but the one that becomes clear on Palm Sunday is that
really coming to terms with the cross means understanding
that the good religious people, you and I, are responsible for
our Lord being there.

Easter cost the greatest price that has ever been paid in the
history of the universe. And yet—miracle of miracles—for us,
Easter is *free.* It cost us nothing; it cost God everything. We did
not deserve God's ultimate sacrifice, but God paid it out of his
vast storehouse of unconditional love. Your tears and mine are
merely sentimental most of the time, but the tears of Jesus are
wrung out of God's inmost heart of yearning compassion. The
Messiah weeps for the sin that brings him to Jerusalem to die
for her redemption. It is our complicity in sin that brings him
there; it is our sin that he bears away from us like the scapegoat
going into the wilderness. He weeps for you and for me. *The
Lord has laid on him the iniquity of us all* (Isa. 53).

What load are you carrying? Bring it to Jesus. He has borne
it already. What secret tears are you bottling up? He knows. He

understands. He is taking it with him as he begins his journey to Calvary. "Shun not suffering, shame, or loss; learn of him to bear the cross."[26]

PRAYER

Almighty and everliving God, who, of thy tender love towards mankind, hast sent thy Son our Savior Jesus Christ to take upon him our flesh, and to suffer death upon the cross, that all mankind should follow the example of his great humility: Mercifully grant that we may both follow the example of his patience, and also be made partakers of his resurrection; through the same Jesus Christ our Lord, who liveth and reigneth with thee and the Holy Spirit, one God, for ever and ever. Amen.

Luke 22:39–46

And being in an agony he prayed more earnestly; and his sweat became like great drops of blood falling down upon the ground.

—LUKE 22:44

Today we're turning our attention to what occurs immediately after the Last Supper. We read that Jesus went out to the Mount of Olives "as was his custom," and the disciples trudged along after him, with—by now—considerable amounts of fear and foreboding. The Master comes to the place he seeks and asks the disciples to wait and pray while he goes some distance farther.

He withdrew from them about a stone's throw, and knelt down and prayed, "Father, if thou art willing, remove this cup from me; nevertheless not my will, but thine, be done." [And there appeared to him an angel from heaven, strengthening him. And being in an agony he prayed more earnestly; and his sweat became like great drops of blood falling down upon the ground.]

Why did Jesus struggle and suffer like this before his death? Matthew, Mark, Luke, and the Epistle to the Hebrews all testify about this great agony that he endured. According to one translation of Saint Mark (J. B. Phillips), he "began to be horror-stricken and desperately depressed"; the Greek is very strong here. In Hebrews we read: "In the days of his flesh, Jesus offered up prayers and supplications, with loud cries and tears, to him who was able to save him from death.... Although he was a Son, he learned obedience through what he suffered" (Heb. 5:7–8). Why do you think Jesus is suffering like this? It can't be just fear of death; many people have gone stoically and fearlessly to their deaths, even vile criminals. Why have the New Testament writers preserved this memory of Jesus agonizing? They could have just omitted it. Instead, they have put special emphasis on it.

Most of us don't know much about crucifixion as a method. Perhaps more than any other form of execution that has ever been devised, this method was designed to degrade. It was done in public places so that everyone could participate in the shaming of the crucified person. That was its purpose: to shame, to humiliate, and finally to dehumanize. What irony! Jesus was the one truly perfect human being, yet the crucifixion method was arranged for the purpose of announcing to the passersby that this object on this cross is not even human.

Crucifixion shows us the ultimate cruelty that lurks in the human heart. This is the way that we managed to put the Son of God to death. Without doubt, from the point of view of the disciples, his crucifixion would mean the total obliteration of his teaching and, more striking still, the extermination of his memory. It can't be said too strongly: this is not the path that religious figures are supposed to travel. This is not an enlightened passage into the higher consciousness; this is not a serene yielding to a warmly enveloping spirit; this is not a radiant light-filled translation to a higher realm. This is an unspeakable ordeal of blood and spittle and mockery and excrement and utmost degradation. Why?

The mystery of the crucifixion can never be entirely grasped by us, but the New Testament witnesses repeatedly testify that it was for sin. The meaning of this terrible method surely lies in the correspondence between the ugliness of the cross and the ugliness of human sin.

Sin is a meaningless concept to those who do not know God. It cannot be defined apart from the holiness and righteousness of the God of Abraham, Isaac, and Jacob, the God and Father of our Lord Jesus Christ. Sin is not disobedience in general, rebellion in general, bad behavior in general. It is disobedience, rebellion, and bad behavior in the sight of God, the God who has made his covenant with us in holiness and righteousness. Therefore—pay attention to this great truth—to know sin is to be already in a state of grace.

Remember these words from Psalm 51, the Ash Wednesday psalm: "I know my transgressions, and my sin is ever before me. Against thee, thee only, have I sinned, and done that which is evil in thy sight, so that thou art justified in thy sentence and blameless in thy judgment." Only a person who really knows God, as King David knew God, can say those words.

So why is Jesus down on his knees in the garden, sweating blood and pleading with his Father? It is because he is preparing to take God's judgment against Sin upon himself. In an important verse, Saint Paul says in Romans 8:3 that God, "sending his own Son in the likeness of sinful flesh and for sin, ... condemned sin in the flesh." We are not able to understand entirely what that means—God condemned sin in the flesh—but it is surely related to what our Lord is facing in his flesh as he agonizes in the Garden of Gethsemane. This is not going to be just a crucifixion, horrible as that is. Incomparably more horrible is the separation from the Father that Jesus will undergo. The Son of God is going to receive in his own body the condemnation of God against Sin, and in so doing, he takes that condemnation away from us. "There is," Saint Paul writes, "therefore now no condemnation for those who are in Christ Jesus" (Rom. 8:1).

God has condemned sin in the flesh of Jesus, and we are free. So our overwhelming response, the motive power behind all Christian action, is gratitude. Gratitude is a very personal motivation. Gratitude arises out of the Holy Week vision of Jesus, not soaring unscathed into realms of light above us and beyond us, untouched by human pain, but down on his knees on the ground, weeping, abandoned, sweating blood, beseeching his Father, preparing to meet Sin and Death disarmed and unprotected, gathering himself for his climactic battle against your Enemy and mine. We cannot achieve freedom from sin and death through our own spiritual striving. The victory is given to us as a present, the free gift achieved for us through the suffering and death of Jesus Christ, the only begotten Son of God.

PRAYER

O God, who by the passion of thy blessed Son didst make an instrument of shameful death to be unto us the means of life: Grant us so to glory in the cross of Christ, that we may gladly suffer shame and loss for the sake of thy Son our Savior Jesus Christ; who liveth and reigneth with thee and the Holy Spirit, one God, for ever and ever. *Amen.*

John 18:1–19:42

> So they took Jesus, and he went out, bearing his own cross, to the place
> called the place of a skull, which is called in Hebrew Golgotha. There
> they crucified him, and with him two others, one on either side, and
> Jesus between them.
>
> —JOHN 19:17–18

On Good Friday, the Christian gospel decisively defines itself. This is the day that differentiates the faith of the church from religion in general. We are so far removed from the gruesome reality of crucifixion as the ancient world knew it that we are scarcely able to imagine its offensiveness, its loathsomeness, its gross unsuitability as an object of religious reverence or worship.

There is a sense in which this instrument of torture is the most irreligious thing that ever was. And yet, as theologian Jürgen Moltmann has written, the cross is "the inner criterion of Christian theology." We simply cannot have a sanitized Christianity.

The reason we read all the very long passion narrative is that we seek to enter into the meaning of this death by state-sanctioned brutality. One thing is certain from the outset: this is not a day for contemplating the suffering of an innocent hero whom we might someday emulate or imitate. If drawn into that frame of reference, we might lose the argument to someone who points out that others have suffered more horribly than Jesus, more stoically and for a longer period.

The biblical writers have forestalled any such discussion by their reticence concerning those very matters. It is not physical suffering that dominates the passion narratives; the evangelists are concerned with the inner meaning of the events. Mark pictures Christ derelict and rejected by God, yet precisely in that condition and at that moment publicly confessed for the first time as the only begotten Son of the Father. Matthew also emphasizes the dereliction and the mockery, but he characteristically shows forth Christ as the Son of David and Messiah of Israel at the same time, bearing high titles, with mighty revelatory signs testifying to the true meaning of his rejected condition. Luke depicts Jesus reigning as King even from the cross, with power to determine the eternal destinies of men ("Today thou shalt be with me in Paradise"); and John interprets the passion and death as the triumph of the Lamb, the "hour of glory" when he wins the victory over death and the devil. These are the themes that the New Testament writers care about.

The passion of Jesus is set in contrast to the behavior of the disciples and the other players in the drama. While the Master is on his way to his trial, torture, and death, everyone else in the story is protecting his own flanks. Judas, Peter, Pontius Pilate, and the disciples are thinking, not of Jesus, but of ways to vindicate themselves. That is precisely the point of difference between Jesus and us. Self-help is the American gospel, which translates into self-congratulation and self-protection.

We Americans excuse our attitudes on the grounds of the American creed: "God helps those who help themselves." This motif is eerily echoed, or parodied, in the taunts flung at Jesus on the cross:

Those who passed by derided him, wagging their heads and saying, "You who would destroy the temple and build it in three days, save yourself! If you are the Son of God,

come down from the cross." So also the chief priests, with
the scribes and elders, mocked him, saying, "He saved others; he cannot save himself. He is the King of Israel; let him
come down now from the cross, and we will believe in him."
(Matt. 27:39–42)

It is easy for us, far removed from the scene, to distance ourselves from these hateful imprecations. Yet something about
them is familiar to us; we expect people to reap what they sow,
to get what they deserve, to make their own luck, to pull themselves up by their own bootstraps. "Is it nothing to you, all you
who pass by?" This verse from Lamentations has traditionally
been associated with Jesus on the cross. The implied answer is,
"Yes, it is nothing to us."

Today we see how the Son of God has entered into the condition of those who cannot save themselves, those who are defenseless, those who deserve to die. This was his free choice.
In Gethsemane, he asked the Father if he might not be spared
this final sentence, this death penalty; he rose from his knees
knowing that he had chosen the path laid out for him since
before the world began. In the garden that night, he shrank
from the sentence of judgment that he did not deserve, but in
the wrestling, in the struggle, in the agony that the disciples
were too weak to share, he submitted to that sentence on our
behalf—so that it would not fall on us. He went forth to arrest,
trial, and execution; he became the Judge judged in our place.
He has written *our death sentence* in *his own blood*, and thereby
has deflected it from us forever.

What is happening today is that we are recapitulating the
story of fall and redemption. We are not just observing it; we
are placing ourselves within it. The great deception that we
human beings practice on ourselves is that we can get ourselves out of the fix we are in—but today we know that we
cannot follow through on it. We look at ourselves today with
the Savior's eyes. Jesus looks at us, and he knows that we cannot help ourselves. He looks at us this very day in the same way

he looked at every human being that he encountered during his earthly life: with infinite sadness for our predicament, yet with unquenchable love and with unflinching resolve to rescue us from certain condemnation and death, whatever it took, wherever it led, whatever the price. "Self-help" is crucified with Christ—for, as Saint Paul writes, "While we were *still helpless*, Christ died for the ungodly" (Rom. 5:6).

To continue Paul's thought in Romans 5 with verses 8–10:

> God shows his love for us in that while we were yet sinners Christ died for us. Since, therefore, we are now justified by his blood, much more shall we be saved by him from the wrath of God. For if while we were enemies we were reconciled to God by the death of his Son, much more, now that we are reconciled, shall we be saved by his life.

So let us humbly thank God on this day of days for his infinite mercy, and let us come to the foot of the cross to praise him for his help when we could not help ourselves. Lord Jesus Christ, my only Savior and Lord, "help of the helpless, O abide with me."

PRAYER

Almighty God, we beseech thee graciously to behold this thy family, for whom our Lord Jesus Christ was contented to be betrayed, and given into the hands of sinners, and to suffer death upon the cross; who now liveth and reigneth with thee and the Holy Spirit, one God, for ever and ever. *Amen.*

EASTER

John 20:1–18

> Now on the first day of the week Mary Magdalene came to the tomb
> early, while it was still dark, and saw that the stone had been taken
> away from the tomb.
>
> —JOHN 20:1

The symbolism of night and darkness pervades the Gospel of John. At the very beginning we hear the proclamation that the light of the incarnate Word of God comes to shine in the darkness (1:5). Repeatedly in this gospel, Jesus teaches that he brings light to the world; without him, it is night. We read that "Jesus spoke to them, saying, 'I am the light of the world; he who follows me will not walk in darkness, but will have the light of life'" (8:12). Most portentously, the master dramatist John tells us in his account of our Lord's last evening on earth that he was "troubled in spirit," saying, "One of you will betray me." He dips a morsel of bread into the wine and gives it to Judas. After the morsel, we are told, "Satan entered into Judas … he immediately went out; *and it was night*" (13:21–30).

It *was night*. This is the night in which Sin and Death reign. In the words of Jesus from Luke's Gospel, "This is your hour, and the power of darkness" (Luke 22:53). The liturgy of Holy Week is designed to show that as Jesus dies, every human hope is obliterated. The realm of darkness appears to be victorious. There is nothing left of the Messiah but the grave. And so we read that Joseph of Arimathea came to Pilate to ask permission to take down the body from the cross. Nicodemus also, we are told, "who had at first come to [Jesus] by night," brought spices for anointing, which were traditionally used in an admittedly vain effort to fend off corruption. They bound the body tightly with the spices wrapped in linen bands, "as is the burial custom of the Jews," and placed it in Joseph's own new tomb (John 19:38–42). This would have been late Friday afternoon. There the corpse lay all during the night and all day during the Sabbath, the day in which all work, including the visiting of tombs, was forbidden.

Jesus has entered the realm of Death. The mythology of the Greeks and Romans is by no means wrong here; the dead must cross over the black waters of the river Styx into the kingdom of darkness from which no one can ever return. The Son of God, by his own permission, has been given over to the realm of night. This is where he has gone. We say in the creed, "He descended into hell." Death rules there. Satan rules there. It is night.

Have you buried someone? If you haven't, you will. You will come to know the cold clasp of death. You will know it in the literal sense, when someone who means the world to you is gone, when you yourself must stare it in the face. You will come to know it in a hundred other ways, as the death of a friendship, the death of a career, the loss of youth, the loss of health, the death of happiness, the death of dreams. It will seem to you like the tomb of hope. This, in part, is what John's Gospel means by *night*. The Gospel of John, chapter 20, verse 1: "On the first day of the week Mary Magdalene came to the tomb early, while it was still dark."

While it was still dark. In the middle of the night. This is the night of the end of human hope. Why does Mary come? Why do any of us go to cemeteries? Regardless of the burial customs, the symbolism is the same. The reign of Death is stark, merciless, irrevocable. I have a dear friend whose daughter died tragically. The rest of the family were determined to scatter the ashes on the beach. He was heartbroken about this, and the family agreed to let him have a small portion of the ashes to bury in the family plot. He told me that he was grateful to have something of her left where, as he put it, "I can go to be with her." These little comforts are the best that we can do to cope with our grief and loss—walking on a beach, sitting by a grave. These are the few shreds of solace that we are able to snatch from the jaws of Death before we, too, disappear.

We are not told why Mary went to the tomb in the middle of the night, but one thing is for sure: she was not expecting the resurrection. So when she came to the tomb in the dark and saw that the stone had been removed, she ran to Peter and the others with the news that Jesus's body had been stolen. What other explanation could there be for an empty tomb? And so the men run to see for themselves.

> The other [younger] disciple outran Peter and reached the tomb first; and stooping to look in, he saw the linen cloths lying there, but he did not go in. Then Simon Peter came, following him, and went into the tomb; he saw the linen cloths lying, and the napkin, which had been on his head, not lying with the linen cloths but rolled up in a place by itself. Then the other disciple, who reached the tomb first, also went in, and he saw and believed; for as yet they did not know the scripture, that he must rise from the dead. (John 20:4–9)

Remember this: the evangelist wants us to know that the resurrection was truly inconceivable. The two disciples did not know what had happened until they got there. It was the sight of the cloths that revealed to them what was otherwise unthinkable. No grave robber would stop to unwrap the winding sheet. Jesus's body had simply passed through them.

The resurrection happened *at night*. No one was there when it happened. When the women and the disciples arrived, he was gone. He arose from the kingdom of Death and carried away its spoils. The rising sun revealed the victory already accomplished. And so the risen, living, reigning Christ says to us today as he said to Martha, "I am the resurrection and the life; whoever believes in me, though he die, yet shall he live, and whoever lives and believes in me shall never die. Do you believe this?" (John 11:25–26).

Let our answer be hers: "Yes, Lord; I believe that you are the Christ, the Son of God"—and in believing, receive the gift of eternal light and life in his name (John 20:30–31).

> *Alleluia! Christ is risen!*
> *The Lord is risen indeed! Alleluia! Alleluia!*

PRAYER

Almighty God, who through thine only-begotten Son Jesus Christ overcame death and opened unto us the gate of everlasting life: Grant that we, who celebrate with joy the day of the Lord's resurrection, may be raised from the death of sin by thy life-giving Spirit; through the same Jesus Christ our Lord, who liveth and reigneth with thee and the same Spirit, one God, now and for ever. Amen.

John 20:19–31

[Jesus] said to Thomas, "Put your finger here, and see my hands; and put out your hand, and place it in my side; do not be faithless, but believing."

—JOHN 20:27

It is a very comforting thing to me, in my own struggle to believe, to know that the relationship of doubt to faith is built into the Easter story. Mark, for instance, deliberately ends his gospel on a note of doubt. Today, the first Sunday after Easter Day, the story of "Doubting Thomas" is always read.

The kind of doubt that is on view today, as we hear the story of Thomas from the Gospel of John, is not trendy disaffection. It is doubt that arises even in the midst of faith. You know the outlines of the narrative. Thomas was not present when Jesus first appeared. When the other disciples report to him that they have seen the Lord, he says that unless he himself touches the wounds in Jesus's hands and side, he will not believe. Thomas stands for all of us here. We haven't seen the risen Lord. We have heard reports, but we don't know how reliable they are. We would like proof. We would like to see evidence that will hold up in the courts of the skeptics.

In 1994, a church in Piedmont, Alabama, was destroyed by a tornado on Palm Sunday morning. Twenty people were killed, including six children. The four-year-old daughter of the pastor was killed. I remember reading about it in the *New York Times* on Easter Sunday. The story was filled with cries of pain. A man looked at the little patent-leather Easter shoes of the children lying in the ruins and said, "If that don't shake your faith, nothing will." A woman said, "We are trained from birth not to question God. But why? Why a church? Why those little children? Why? Why? Why?" The Reverend Kelly Clem, mother of the four-year-old, said, "We do not know why. I don't think 'why' is the question right now. We just have to help each other through it."

Surely it is of the utmost importance that the sign demanded by Thomas was to touch the marks of Jesus's *wounds*. It was not the sign of his glory that gave proof, but the sign of his sufferings. Again and again this brings us back to the place where faith must stand—not in the place of clarity and certainty, but in the place of ambiguity and pain. Thomas's choice of signs is surely related to Jesus's amazing consent to his demand. Jesus says to Thomas, "Put your finger here, and see my hands; and put out your hand, and place it in my side; do not be faithless, but believing" (John 20:27). Interpreters tend to agree that Thomas never actually touches Jesus; the appearance of the Master, the sight of his wounds, and his word are enough. In the final analysis, it is the Word of Jesus that creates faith.

In the beginning of our reading for today from the Gospel of John, Thomas is in the same position that you and I are in. He has not seen the risen Lord. His reaction is one of disbelief. We are accustomed to hearing stories of Jesus turning away from people who will not believe without a sign, so it is startling when he graciously appears to Thomas and grants him the proofs that he demanded. At this climactic moment, Thomas utters a confession of faith that is the most exalted in all the New Testament. He uses words that the Old Testament reserves exclusively for the one and only Creator God of the universe, "My Lord and my God."

The story about Thomas is placed by the evangelist John at the apex of his gospel story for a specific reason. Neither you nor I have seen the risen Lord with our own eyes as Thomas did, but our faith is founded on his Word, living and active as it is proclaimed today on the second Sunday of the Easter season. That is why Jesus says, "Blessed are they who do not see and yet believe" (John 20:29).

We have a real choice. We can choose a god who suits us in every particular because he is a projection of ourselves, whose voice is essentially our own voice magnified. This god will have no nail prints in his hands. This goddess will have no wound in her side. If we don't like the tornadoes and premature deaths and other things that happen in the world, we can absolve our man-made gods from responsibility, since they are *part of* the world and not *creators* of it.

The Bible sets before us a baffling, even an infuriating God who is really God, rather than a domesticated household pet. Our God is a God who permits us to doubt, to complain, to shake our fist, to shout at him, to ask repeatedly the ultimate question, "Why?" Ultimately the divine answer does not come in the form of a "why." It comes in the form of a "Who." Even in the midst of pain, grief, and doubt, I believe we can hold on to the promise that God has entered our pain and been wounded by it, actually been killed by it, yet has been raised triumphant from the dead never to die again, having power to grant his divine life to all who come to him. And we proclaim to you today not our own voice but the living Word of God, which is unique and trustworthy. When Thomas makes his confession, Jesus says to him, "Thomas, have you believed because you have seen me?" Then the Lord looks straight through Thomas, across and down the centuries to the believers and doubters yet to come, to you and to me: "Blessed are they who do not see and yet believe" (John 20:29).

"These things were written that you may believe that Jesus is the Christ, the Son of God, and that, believing, you may have life in his name" (v. 31).

PRAYER

O God, who by the glorious resurrection of thy Son Jesus Christ
destroyed death and brought life and immortality to light:
Grant that we, who have been raised with him, may abide in
his presence and rejoice in the hope of eternal glory; through
the same Jesus Christ our Lord, to whom, with thee and the
Holy Spirit, be dominion and praise for ever and ever. *Amen.*

Job 38; 42:1–6

> "I have uttered what I did not understand,
>   things too wonderful for me, which I did not know."

—JOB 42:3

Today's text comes from the very end of the book of Job. Job is the man who has lost everything: home, business, family. And now he has a hideous skin disease. Job's friends come to comfort him, but the more they talk, the more Job resists them and their pious platitudes. Job endures their windy words as long as he can, and then he makes his last-ditch stand. The sum of his passionate outcries is a demand that God respond to him.

Well, God responds. God appears out of a whirlwind and addresses Job directly. When this happens, the result is astonishing: Job simply sets aside all his great sufferings and abandons all the many words he has spoken.

> "I have uttered what I did not understand,
>   things too wonderful for me, which I did not know."
>   (42:3)

After this, Job speaks no more. His mouth is stopped.

> "I had heard of thee by the hearing of the ear,
>   but now my eye sees thee;

therefore I despise myself,
   and repent in dust and ashes." (42:5–6)

One respected modern translator puts it this way: "I will be quiet, comforted that I am dust."[27] This makes the point best. What happens to Job is some sort of radical, life-changing humility before God. That's what the book means. God has come to meet Job, and nothing is the same after that. Job has demanded an answer from God, and God has answered him.

God's answer is no answer at all, and yet, much to the mystification of the modern reader, Job seems more than satisfied. His response is so dramatically different from anything that he has been saying before that the careful listener is stunned into silence along with him as he says,

"I have uttered what I did not understand,
   …things too wonderful for me, which I did not know.…
I had heard of you with my ears,
   …but now my eyes have seen you.
Therefore I will be quiet,
   …comforted that I am dust."[28]

The season of Lent began on Ash Wednesday, eight weeks ago, with these traditional words: "Dust thou art, and unto dust thou shalt return." Today, on this high holy day of the Easter season, we hear the words "I am comforted that I am dust." We human beings begin and end in dust. In the creation story from Genesis we read that the Lord God formed Adam from the dust of the earth. You don't have to reject evolutionary science to understand the symbolic meaning of this. As Saint Paul says, the first man, Adam, was "a man of dust" (1 Cor. 15:47). Ashes to ashes. Dust we are, and to dust we return.

Virtually all interpreters agree that the book of Job gives no answer at all to the problem of suffering. The voice out of the whirlwind passes over it altogether. What God says is, basically, this: "Job, can you create the world that I have created? Look at it! Look at the wonderful things I have made—the snow and the rain, the stars in the firmament, the doors of the sea. Can you make the sun blaze in the heavens or the planets move in their orbits? Can you even imagine, let alone create, all the amazing beasts of the field and the sea? If you can do that, then surely you don't need me; your own flesh and blood can save you!"

The book of Job is asking this great question: Is there a living God beyond what we can imagine? Is there a Being independent of us, beyond the boundaries of earthly life and earthly struggle? Is there a God who speaks with a voice that is not simply projected out of our human religious consciousness? Is there a God who can deliver us from the dust? Job's great longing is for *revelation*. He craves a God who is really God. He wants to be shown that God has a power that he cannot discern in the world that he knows.[29] That is why he is different from his friends, whose entire message is bound up with their need to believe that there are "explanations" for everything.

Now if God had answered Job in the way that we would expect, with soothing explanations and comforting reassurances, then the answer to the question "Is there a God beyond what we can imagine?" would have to be no. Anyone can imagine a God who does what we expect. The reason that so many people have complained that God's answer to Job is no answer at all is that they want a God who fits their preconceptions. Job, however, is manifestly satisfied. The God who is really God has come to him and has revealed himself as the one who was already present, already powerful, already at work before there was anyone to imagine him. God is the author of creation; the creation is not the author of God. This was revealed to Job by the living voice and presence of God's own self. That was enough.

Last week we read in the Gospel of John that the disciple Thomas wasn't interested in hearing what the other disciples had to say about the resurrection. Very much like Job, he refused to be satisfied until he got a personal response from the Son of God. If he didn't get one, he would not believe. When Jesus therefore came and stood before him, Thomas hushed up in the same way that Job did, and for the same reason: God had revealed himself from a domain beyond the grave that Thomas could not have imagined for himself. The living Son of God had appeared to him personally. Thomas's response is the pinnacle of Christian affirmation, spoken in the highest language of the Bible: *My Lord and my God.*

I have uttered what I did not understand, things too wonderful for me, which I did not know.... The message of the resurrection is indeed too wonderful for us. Flesh and blood cannot inherit it. It is grasped only by faith. Through the Word of God the Holy Spirit creates such faith in those who gladly hear the message.

PRAYER

O God, whose blessed Son did manifest himself to his disciples in the breaking of bread: Open, we pray thee, the eyes of our faith, that we may behold him in all his redeeming work; through the same thy Son Jesus Christ our Lord, who liveth and reigneth with thee, in the unity of the Holy Spirit, one God, now and for ever. *Amen.*

John 10:11–30

"*I am the good shepherd. The good shepherd lays down his life for the sheep.*"

—JOHN 10:11

One of the hardest things about being a preacher and teacher in our time is that biblical memory almost no longer exists in the Western church. It is impossible to re-create the situation of those who first heard Jesus's words "I am the good shepherd." All the same, we have to try, because if we do, we will begin to see that it is not just a warm and fuzzy concept but also a reality of incomparable power.

The shepherd image was deeply embedded in the living faith of Israel. There are a number of important passages in the Old Testament that portray God as the shepherd of his people. That may sound ho-hum to you and me, but it was electrifying for those who, after the resurrection, remembered how Jesus had spoken of himself. Listen to this crucial passage from Ezekiel, remembering that it was written when the people had been sent into miserable exile in heathen Babylon:

> "For thus says the Lord God: Behold, I, I myself will search for my sheep, and will seek them out. As a shepherd seeks out his flock when some of his sheep have been scattered abroad, so will I seek out my sheep; and I will rescue them.... I will seek the lost, and I will bring back the strayed, and I will

\[CODE\]

bind up the crippled.... [For] you are my sheep, the sheep of my pasture, and I am your God, says the Lord God." (Ezek. 34:11–12, 16, 31)

It is not easy for us to appropriate the impact of such a passage, and many others like it, upon the collective memory of a people who had been living for centuries under the rule of first one and then another colossal, overwhelming pagan culture. We just have to try to imagine what it meant to them to know that in spite of everything there were these promises that the Lord would bring them home again, restore their losses to them, and shelter them from every evil.

With this little bit of background, it is perhaps possible to glimpse the impact of the way Jesus talks about himself. In the New Testament, the motif of the shepherd—remarkably— is no longer used to refer to God the Father. The imagery has shifted entirely to Jesus. This is true in all four Gospels, but it is most obvious in John's Gospel: "I am the good shepherd; I know my own and my own know me.... My sheep hear my voice, and I know them, and they follow me; and I give them eternal life, and they shall never perish.... No one is able to snatch them out of the Father's hand. I and my Father are one" (John 10:14, 27–30).

So, you see, these are not just sweet sayings about what a kind and loving person Jesus is. Everybody who knew the Jewish Scriptures knew that *only God* was able to fulfill the promises made through the prophet Ezekiel; therefore this utterance, "I am the good shepherd," makes Jesus equal to God, and the final clincher just nails that into place: "I and my Father are one."

What does this mean?

It means that ultimate power and ultimate love are united in one person. Let's think about that. Everybody knows about the data that has come in about children in orphanages in places where they are not touched or held or talked to. We know that human beings cannot thrive without love. What is less generally acknowledged is that powerlessness is very bad for us. Powerlessness produces anger, which produces paralyzing depression at one end of the spectrum, and at the other, murderous violence.

We are much less likely to admit the ill effects of powerlessness than those of lovelessness. After all, giving love doesn't sound threatening. Granting power is another matter. All around the world, Christians on the top of the socioeconomic heap have talked endlessly about love while preventing people of a lower bracket from having any power. Power to the powerless is an infinitely threatening idea because it might mean that you and I have to give up some of it.

In the Good Shepherd, power and love meet. If the shepherd loves the sheep but cannot protect them, the image becomes merely sentimental. Any parent will understand this, because every parent must inevitably learn what it is like to be unable to protect a child from illness, or accident, or false choices. Faith cannot protect us or our children from the sorrows of life; but there is a reason that study after study shows that people of faith cope better in times of trouble. The reason is that a decision to trust Jesus is a form of reempowerment.

"I am the good shepherd. . . . My sheep hear my voice, and I know them, and they follow me; and I give them eternal life, and they shall never perish, and no one shall snatch them out of my hand" (John 10:14, 27–28). And Jesus continues, in words that have no parallel in religious literature: "I lay down my life for the sheep. . . . For this reason the Father loves me, because I lay down my life, that I may take it again. No one takes it from me, but I lay it down of my own accord. I have power to lay it down, and I have power to take it again; this charge I have received from my Father" (vv. 15, 17–18).

Here is the power, and here is the love. Do you see how the love between God the Father and God the Son issues forth in love so great that it gives itself up for the sheep? Life for the sheep comes through the death of the Shepherd. But that is not the end. Good Friday is not the end. "I have power to lay it down, and I have power to take it again; this charge I have received from my Father." The dominion of Death is blown to bits on Easter Day. The Good Shepherd is not dead. He is alive and speaking tenderly to you now. "I know my own, and my own know me."

Jesus, the Good Shepherd: he alone is the loving and powerful One who is able to secure the safety and the fulfillment and the eternal destiny of his beloved children forever and ever, our Father and our Mother, the Resurrection and the Life, our Lord and our God.

PRAYER

O God, whose Son Jesus is the good shepherd of thy people; Grant that when we hear his voice we may know him who calleth us each by name, and follow where he doth lead; who, with thee and the Holy Spirit, liveth and reigneth, one God, for ever and ever. *Amen.*

FIFTH SUNDAY OF EASTER

1 Corinthians 15

I delivered to you as of first importance what I also received, that Christ died for our sins in accordance with the scriptures, that he was buried, that he was raised on the third day in accordance with the scriptures.

—1 CORINTHIANS 15:3-4

I remember reading a review of a book called *The Bible Unearthed.*[30] Written by two leading archaeologists, it is about the latest discoveries being dug up in the biblical lands and what these finds might mean for the interpretation of the Scriptures. Things have changed since I was in theological school. In the 1950s and '60s when I first started studying the Bible, we were constantly being cheered on by the latest news from the digs. The more the archaeologists uncovered, we were told, the more their finds corroborated the stories of the biblical ancestors—Abraham, Moses, Joshua, David.

Now the whole thing has been reversed. To the great delight of the Bible-debunkers, the stories in the first part of the Old Testament cannot be shown to be historically dependable. The exodus did not happen as described; the swift conquest of Canaan never took place; the great King Solomon was probably just a local tribal chieftain. The authors of *The Bible Unearthed*, according to this review, show great reverence for the Hebrew Bible, but (they believe) it is "not a miraculous revelation, but a brilliant product of the human imagination."

It all reminds me of the words of the Gershwin song, "The things that you're liable to read in the Bible / It ain't necessarily so."

Now let's fast-forward to the New Testament. The text for today is the fifteenth chapter of the first letter of the apostle Paul to the Christians in the city of Corinth. Paul was very worried about the Corinthian Christians. They were drifting away from the path of truth and life. Paul writes to call them back. He begins chapter 15 with these words: "Now I would remind you, brothers and sisters, in what terms I preached to you the gospel, which you received, in which you stand, by which you are saved, if you hold it fast—unless you believed in vain." In this climactic chapter—one of the most powerful passages that he ever wrote—Paul is saying, This is it, Corinthians. It's this or nothing. What I proclaimed to you as good news is nothing less than the salvation of the world, unless you want to throw it away. Everything—*everything*—depends on whether I told you the truth or not.

In the next two or three sentences, Paul sums up the Christian message that he preached everywhere he went. "I delivered to you as of first importance what I also received, that Christ died for our sins in accordance with the scriptures, that he was buried, that he was raised on the third day in accordance with the scriptures, and that he appeared to Cephas [Peter], then to the twelve [disciples, later apostles]."

We need to notice several things about this summary of the gospel message. First, you will see that Paul does not offer religious ideas, inspirational sayings, or "spiritual" lessons. He simply declares that *something happened*. He describes it in four sentences:

Jesus Christ died.
He was dead and buried.
On the third day he was raised from the dead.
He appeared to his disciples.

This is the message that converted the Mediterranean world and that is still creating new Christians around the globe. It is not a collection of generic religious principles. It is an announcement about *events that happened* and that can be described: Christ died; Christ was buried; Christ was raised from the dead; Christ appeared, living, to his disciples.

A second thing to notice is that Paul says twice, "in accordance with the scriptures." Twice in one sentence he says it. Apparently this is very important to him. He wants the connection between Jesus Christ and the God of the Old Testament nailed into place. He wants us to know that the God of Abraham, Isaac, and Jacob is the same God who is the Father of Jesus Christ and that the whole thing was planned from the beginning. And, clearly, he thinks that the Scripture can be trusted. If David and Solomon were not exactly the mighty rulers that live in song and story, that is not the point. The point is that God was at work in them, and in the entire history of Israel, "with a mighty hand and an outstretched arm."

Now we come to verses 12 through 17. This passage is well known, but I don't know if you've noticed the uncompromising do-or-die, either-or quality of it. Again, we can break down the argument to its simplest components:

> If there is no resurrection of the dead, then Christ has not been raised.
> If Christ has not been raised, then the apostles' preaching is in vain.
> If Christ has not been raised, your faith is futile and you are still in your sins.

Let us be realistic. The point of view expressed in the book review is now so widely held—even within the church—that it is a full-time job to plug even one hole in the dike. Yet every sermon, every exposition of a biblical text is a precious opportunity to strike a blow against the prevailing fashion of regarding the Holy Scriptures as the product of human imagination. Let Paul speak again: "I delivered to you as of first importance what I also received, that Christ died for our sins in accordance with the scriptures, that he was buried, that he was raised on the third day in accordance with the scriptures." Does that sound to you like a man who is in love with his own imagination? Or is it not rather a man who is reporting, not amorphous religious ideas, but the most important thing that has ever happened?

Paul declared the Word of God two thousand years ago as I now declare it to you today. The inexorability of Death has been reversed; its remorselessness has been overcome; its effects have been undone. We see this now by faith; in the resurrection day we shall see it face-to-face. But be assured: it is not "necessarily" so. It is not so because we want it to be so, because we imagine it to be so, because we need it to be so. It is so *against* all human possibility, *against* all human expectation, *against* all human imagining. It is so by the miraculous intervention of our God, who has not abandoned us to the grave.

PRAYER

O Almighty God, whom truly to know is everlasting life: Grant us so perfectly to know thy Son Jesus Christ to be the way, the truth, and the life, that we may steadfastly follow his steps in the way that leadeth to eternal life; through the same thy Son Jesus Christ our Lord, who liveth and reigneth with thee, in the unity of the Holy Spirit, one God, for ever and ever. Amen.

SIXTH SUNDAY OF EASTER

Psalm 16; John 10:1–18

Thou dost show me the path of life;
  in thy presence there is fulness of joy,
  in thy right hand are pleasures for evermore.

—PSALM 16:11

The more we know of life, the more we experience its disappointments and sorrows, the more we learn that things don't work out the way we wanted, the more the Bible has to offer us. The people of the Bible are not stained-glass figures; they are like us. They are flesh and blood. They turn away from God, make deals with crooks, stab people in the back. They complain, argue, cheat, commit adultery, tell lies. They suffer; they are struck down in war, felled by disease, exploited by oppressors. Their children die, their homes are destroyed, their crops are eaten by plagues of locusts. But here is the central fact. All this happens in the sight of God and in the context of his faithfulness. That's why we often find two seemingly contradictory things in the same psalm, for instance, in Psalm 40: "Though I am poor and afflicted, the Lord will have regard for me." Or Psalm 38: "My loins are filled with searing pain, there is no health in my body; I am utterly numb and crushed … [but] in you, Lord, have I fixed my hope; you will answer me, O Lord my God."

How can the Psalms be so filled with despair and hope at the same time? Is this what is frequently called "the triumph of the human spirit"?

No, it isn't. One of the central truths of biblical faith is that the human spirit, left to itself, is doomed to self-destruct. The biblical man, or woman, does not say, "I am the master of my soul, I am the captain of my fate." We do not say, "I did it my way." We do not lift our heads pridefully in our own strength. Instead, we say with the psalmist, "You, O Lord, are a shield about me; you are my glory, the one who lifts up my head" (Ps. 3:3).

"Thou dost show me the path of life; in thy presence there is fulness of joy, in thy right hand are pleasures for evermore." Is it true? Or is it just wishful thinking, like so much else that goes on in life? How can we believe this when all the evidence is against it? Let us turn now to the New Testament, the tenth chapter of the Gospel of John, where we find the words of our Lord, speaking as the Good Shepherd: "The thief comes only to steal and kill and destroy [the sheep]; I have come that they might have life, and that they might have it abundantly." This phrase, "abundant life," has captured the imagination of Christians for two thousand years. "In thy presence there is *fulness of joy!*" Can this be trusted?

The story of what God has done for us in Jesus Christ is so huge that words such as "fulness" and "abundance" can never be any more than hints. Another hint that Paul uses a lot in Ephesians is "riches" (Greek *ploutos*). He writes ecstatically about "the riches of his glorious inheritance" (Eph. 1:18), "the immeasurable riches of God's grace" (2:7), "the unsearchable riches of Christ" (3:8). These are his best attempts to say the unsayable. God has promised us the abundance of his own inexhaustible riches, not because we deserved them—Scripture teaches us we most decidedly did not deserve them—but because it was his purpose to give them to us out of his unbounded, indeed immeasurable, love.

But what a strange story it is that the church tells! God did not come in the form of riches, or wealth, or worldly power. Saint Paul puts it another way: "You know the grace of our Lord Jesus Christ, that though he was rich, yet for your sake he became poor, so that by his poverty you might become rich" (2 Cor. 8:9). So it is a paradox, isn't it? God's riches are made known to us in a hidden way. In order to make us rich he became poor. In order to lift up our heads he lowered his own. In order to give us abundant life he "became subject to evil and death."[31] In doing all this he enacted for us the way to be human before God—obedient and submissive to the Father, yet defiant and unbowed before the Enemy, which is Sin and Death.

"In thy presence is fulness of joy.... I have come that they may have life, and may have it abundantly.... I am the Resurrection and the life [says the Lord]; he who believes in me, even though he die, yet shall he live; and he who lives and believes in me shall never die" (John 11:25–26). There is much here that we do not yet understand. Are these promises about the future, or are they supposed to be true already? The answer is, both. When the psalmist sang, "*In thy presence is fulness of joy*," he meant right then and there, in the worship of God. When the ancient Israelite entered the temple to worship, that in itself was *fulness of joy*.

But we know that suffering in this life can be so great that a phrase like "the fulness of joy" can seem like nothing better than a mockery. That is why the Christian community is so indispensable. When we can't pray, the community prays for us. When we have no hope, the community holds the hope for us. When our suffering seems more than we can bear, the community comes alongside us in mute witness. From the standpoint of this vale of tears, we can experience this fulness of joy only in the form of promise. It is not yet, but it will come. We know it now only by faith. But it is not "only" by faith, because, as Paul writes in Romans 5:1–5, the faith and grace "in which we stand" give us the strength we need: "Suffering produces endurance, and endurance produces character, and character produces hope, and *hope does not disappoint us*, because God's love has been poured into our hearts through the Holy Spirit which has been given to us."

Christian hope cannot disappoint us because it is rooted and grounded in the resurrection and guaranteed by the gift of the Spirit. The promise of abundant life, the hope of glory, the guarantee of the fulness of joy lie in our recollection of the mighty act of God, who raised Jesus from the dead and has promised that we will be raised with him. We trust him for the future because in our own day we have heard afresh the ancient Easter message: "The Lord is risen! The Lord is risen indeed! Alleluia!"

PRAYER

O God, who hast prepared for those who love thee such good things as pass man's understanding: Pour into our hearts such love towards thee, that we, loving thee in all things and above all things, may obtain thy promises, which exceed all that we can desire; through Jesus Christ our Lord, who liveth and reigneth with thee and the Holy Spirit, one God, for ever and ever. Amen.

SEVENTH SUNDAY OF EASTER

1 John 1

That which was from the beginning, which we have heard, which we have seen with our eyes, which we have looked upon and touched with our hands ...

—1 JOHN 1:1

The New Testament church found itself in the midst of a society that, like ours, was mixed up about the importance of the human body. Many early Christians did not know what to think. The popular religious beliefs of that day, as of our day, were very tempting. Surely it was more "spiritual" to think of the body as being on a lower plane of existence. One could not really expect to find the presence of the divine in human flesh; it would be distasteful somehow, unworthy, beneath God's dignity. It would compromise the deity to be trapped in something so corruptible, so material, so earthy, so—well, so *fleshy*.

In particular, this was an issue of critical importance with regard to Jesus of Nazareth, a man who was now being hailed by the young, new church as Messiah, as King, as Lord. It was claimed of him that he was the Son of God *incarnate* (from the Latin: *in carno, carnis*, "flesh"). Could this be believed?

The First Epistle of John was apparently written to a church that was split into hostile factions, some maintaining that Jesus was God in human flesh and others insisting that he was not—that God could not possibly have come in real flesh. The

139

opposition said that it *looked* as though he did, but he didn't really. It *seemed* like a body, but that was an illusion. The underlying conviction of these gnostic opponents was the age-old "religious" belief, still alive and well today, that bodily life was of a lesser order than "spiritual" life. This was directly counter to the Hebrew conviction that there isn't any such thing as real human life without a body.

So the author of our Epistle for today wrote a message to counteract this confusion and to set perplexed Christians straight on what the incarnation really was. Our reading for today is a fascinating passage on many levels. It's somewhat garbled in Greek and difficult to translate into English, but the basic message is clear: God's life has appeared in the world in Jesus Christ, in a form that could be heard, seen, and touched. In another passage from this same letter, the author drives the point home: "Beloved, do not believe every spirit, but test the spirits to see whether they are of God; for many false prophets have gone out into the world. By this you know the Spirit of God: every spirit which confesses that Jesus Christ has come in *the flesh* is of God, and every spirit which does not thus confess Jesus is not of God" (4:1–3).

We are forcefully reminded of the Christian proclamation of the resurrection of the *body*, as we say in the Apostles' Creed. To this day there is great resistance to the doctrine of the resurrection of the body in general, and the resurrection of Christ in particular. This resistance isn't just doubt that such a thing happened. It's also because it seems so "unspiritual." Surely, what we call "life after death" isn't so mundane and prosaic as to include muscle and bone, lymph glands and blood vessels— not to mention what Saint Paul calls "the less honorable parts of the body" (1 Cor. 12:23). To be sure, Paul makes it clear in his teaching about the resurrection that our bodies will be *changed*; they will be different, as Jesus's body was different. Yet the New Testament message of the resurrection is one that takes bodily life seriously. There are early Renaissance paintings of heaven, not as naive as they might look; what they show is not a bunch of white-gowned, winged figures floating about in the clouds, but a group of recognizable human beings, grabbing each other, hugging each other, fairly knocking one another's hats off for joy.

Bodies matter. They are not to be treated casually or disposably. The ultimate proof that bodies matter is that Jesus had one. Jesus didn't just come and inhabit a human body for a while, sloughing it off when he was finished with it. He actually became united to our mortal condition. He became a bloody dead body, publicly displayed as unwanted rubbish—that's exactly what crucifixion was supposed to indicate. He became one with our condition in his total nakedness and helplessness.

The Christian claim that the eternal Creator God paid the penalty for our sin in his human flesh remains unique in all the world. But now let us ask ourselves what good it really does in the last analysis to believe this. The extraordinary message of the New Testament is that Jesus has not just entered our condition in order to die alongside us. He has not entered into bodily human life merely in order to share it with us. In entering human flesh, he has actually overcome the enemy. He has won the definitive and final victory over all the ills that flesh is heir to. Saint Paul declares, "As we are united with him in his death, so we shall be united with him in his resurrection" (Rom. 6:5).

The gospel depends on this; a Jesus without flesh and blood is not the Lord and Savior of Christian faith. Faith is the right word. The truth of the resurrection of our Lord is apprehended in this life only by faith. It has immediate and practical consequences. It makes a difference in how we live and how we die.

Years ago I went to a wonderful museum in Birmingham, Alabama, that tells the story of the civil rights movement, and the role of the Christian gospel in it. When the demonstrators and protesters sang "We Shall Overcome," it was with the unconquerable faith that the overcoming of oppression derives its strength from the overcoming of Jesus. The victory of the resurrection is enacted over and over again in the flesh-and-blood conflicts of this present world. That includes you and me in our own mundane struggles against such things as bitterness, resentment, impatience, envy, small-mindedness. In spite of all the ambiguity and vulnerability of our fleshly nature, we are precious in the Lord's sight. For us he has assumed that vulnerability; for us he has undergone its consequences; for us he has been raised out of the grave. On behalf of all victims and hostages everywhere, including ourselves in all our various bondages, let us in heart and mind embrace the wounded hands and feet of our dear Master and Savior, Jesus Christ, our Lord and our God. "As we are united with him in his death, so also shall we be united with him in his resurrection."

PRAYER

O God, who for our redemption didst give thine only-begotten Son to the death of the cross, and by his glorious resurrection hast delivered us from the power of our enemy: Grant us so to die daily to sin, that we may evermore live with him in the joy of his resurrection; through Jesus Christ thy Son our Lord, who liveth and reigneth with thee and the Holy Spirit, one God, now and for ever. *Amen.*

Isaiah 32

The Spirit is poured upon us from on high.

—ISAIAH 32:15

If you're like me, you find that the Holy Spirit is a much harder reality to grasp than God the Father or God the Son. The Creator we know; Jesus Christ we know. But the Holy Spirit seems more elusive.

Last week I undertook a study of all the Old Testament references to the Holy Spirit. Here's what I found. I found *verbs*. Every time the Spirit of God is mentioned in the Old Testament, it's connected to all kinds of active, powerful verbs. We read in the books of Judges and Samuel many times that the Spirit of God "came mightily" upon a person. It didn't just *come*; it came *mightily*. Ezekiel says that "the Spirit entered into me and set me upon my feet" (3:24). This Spirit is a mover. When the Spirit shows up, things happen. As you probably know, the word for "spirit" in Hebrew—*ruach*—also means "breath" or "wind." But this isn't just any old breath. This is the power that brought the creation itself into being out of nothing (creation *ex nihilo*). The first mention of the Spirit of God is in the first chapter of Genesis. Here's the familiar translation from the King James Version:

> In the beginning God created the heaven and the earth. And the earth was without form, and void; and darkness was upon

the face of the deep. And the Spirit of God moved upon the face of the waters. (1:1–2)

But it can also be translated this way: "a mighty wind from God *swept over*" the waters (NRSV alternate). "Swept over" is more forceful than "moved." The Spirit is "mightily" active to create the world "in the beginning." I hope it isn't necessary to say that this is metaphorical truth, not literal truth. The point is this: however the world came into being, God did it.

It's right to say that the Spirit of God, the breath or wind of God, is the *energy* of God. This energy, this power, gives life to all things. God is not waiting around for us to develop our spirituality or our "human potential." God is the one with the life-giving potency. He is at work "mightily," whether we are ready or not. He is bringing things into being that did not exist before, things that are not dependent on us or created by us. Sometimes the Spirit does things that most of us don't even recognize until they've been accomplished.

Isaiah has a great deal to say about the Spirit of God, as in our reading from chapter 32. Notice the key verb there: the Spirit will be *poured out* from on high. The subject of the verb is God. The passage doesn't say a thing about what human beings are going to do; it says that God is going to pour out his Spirit on his people even though they clearly do not deserve it. The passage speaks of effects and results; these are not the results and effects of human activity, but the blessings of the Spirit.

The thing to notice in all of Isaiah's passages about the work of the Spirit of God is that *God's power alone* is able to make restoration possible. We human beings cannot do this by ourselves. There is no true justice, righteousness, or peace unless it is given by God. All of us who have safe beds to sleep in should be thanking God every hour of the day. The "quiet resting places" that God promises are not our due; we are not entitled to them; they are his gift, the outpouring of his Spirit. If you and I are resting or shirking or slacking, his Spirit is nevertheless on the move with somebody else somewhere else, for "behold, he that keepeth Israel shall neither slumber nor sleep" (Ps. 121:4). God is always accomplishing his purposes. God is a verb, and the Spirit of God is a verb. The Spirit is not like "spirituality," which, being a noun, just sort of sits there waiting for us to do something with it. God is not waiting. His creative energy is inexhaustible.

Listen to the verbs in this passage from Isaiah 44:

> "Hear this, O Jacob my servant,
>   Israel whom I have *chosen*!
> Thus says the Lord who *made* you,
>   who *formed* you from the womb and *will help* you:
> Fear not, O Jacob my servant....
> For I *will pour* water on the thirsty land,
>   and streams on the dry ground;
> I *will pour my Spirit* upon your descendants,
>   and my blessing on your offspring.
> *They shall spring up* like grass amid waters,
>   like willows by flowing streams." (44:1–4)

All this activity is the Lord's. He will do these things, and it will be accomplished by the outpouring of the Spirit.

Where is the Holy Spirit at work in the church and world today? There are significant challenges occurring around the world—civil rights, climate change, torture. Each of us must discern the signs of the times and make a decision. Not to make a decision is to make one. Whither blows the Spirit of God?

Maybe you are not up for considering global issues right now. Maybe you had a hard time just getting out of bed this morning. Maybe your marriage is on the rocks. Maybe someone you love is gravely ill. Maybe you are worried about your future. Maybe you are tired of the role you feel you have to play in order to measure up to somebody else's expectations. Maybe your faith is exhausted. Here's a message for you today.

You are not saved by your spirituality or by your anything else. You have been and you will be saved by God. The Holy Spirit of God is your friend. The Holy Spirit is the love of God reaching out for you when you are too depressed, or too angry, or too tired to reach out. The Holy Spirit is the power of God to set you on your feet when you feel you cannot stand up. Forget your own spirituality. We are talking about *God* today, the force that created the universe yet comes to you personally and intimately with an everlasting and unconditional love whether you believe it or not.

PRAYER

O God, who on this day didst teach the hearts of thy faithful people by sending to them the light of thy Holy Spirit: Grant us by the same Spirit to have a right judgment in all things, and evermore to rejoice in his holy comfort; through the merits of Christ Jesus our Savior, who liveth and reigneth with thee, in the unity of the same Spirit, one God, world without end. *Amen.*

SEASON
AFTER
PENTECOST

2 Corinthians 13

The grace of the Lord Jesus Christ and the love of God and the fellow-ship of the Holy Spirit be with you all.

—2 CORINTHIANS 13:14

I magine for a moment that you are the parent of a child, or young person, who appears to be on the verge of self-destruction. Maybe he is hooked on drugs and failing in school, maybe she is anorexic and starving herself, maybe he has run away from home. You are like most parents—you would do anything, anything at all, to reverse the situation. You would spend huge amounts of money for professional help; you would fly across the country; you would pay a ransom, mortgage the house, go without sleep, neglect your own health, jeopardize your standing in the community, throw yourself on the mercy of anyone you thought might intervene. You are desperate. You would make a complete fool of yourself if you thought it might get your child's attention.

This is the position in which the apostle Paul finds himself at the end of his second letter to the Christians in Corinth. The Corinthian church has gone completely off the rails and, furthermore, is on the verge of rejecting him as their leader and teacher. He is planning a trip to Corinth, but trips in those days took months, and he knows that by the time he gets there it might be too late. In desperation he writes an impassioned, erratic letter to the congregation, trying first one tack and then another. The last four chapters of 2 Corinthians form the most agonized portion of the New Testament. One commentator called it almost too painful to read. It is crabbed, tumultuous, disjointed, wildly uneven. Like a parent agonizing because a child has fallen in with a fast crowd, Paul will try almost any argument to see if he can somehow rebuild trust and affection.

When Paul signs off from this letter, he does so with a Trinitarian formula that is well known to us all: "The grace of the Lord Jesus Christ and the love of God and the fellowship of the Holy Spirit be with you all." At first glance it sounds a bit tired and formulaic to us, because we have heard it so many hundreds of times. However, we need to compare this benediction at the end of 2 Corinthians with those in his other letters. The one that we read today is the longest, richest, and fullest of all his valedictory blessings. Usually he says, "The grace of our Lord Jesus be with you" (1 Cor. 16:23). Even to his best-beloved Philippians he says simply, "the grace of our Lord Jesus Christ be with your spirit" (Phil. 4:23). Now, therefore, we are ready to see that Paul was not being perfunctory after all. The church that was breaking his heart is the one that gets the full Trinitarian blessing.

Here we begin to move into the heart of the Trinity: our three-personed God is unique as self-giving love. The inmost being of God is a dynamic interrelatedness that pours itself out for the other without ceasing. It is not dependent on the worthiness of the other, or the response of the other, or the tractability of the other. God's love spends itself to the very last drop of the blood of the Son. As Paul wrote to the Corinthians in one of his previous letters, the love of God "bears all things, believes all things, hopes all things, endures all things" (1 Cor. 13:7).

Reflect on your own life. Think about those people who have borne with you. Think of the people who have loved you and stuck with you in spite of everything. Think of those who did not seem to have much self-regard as they poured all their resources into you, even if you were ungrateful and unresponsive. Think of how, when you were at your very worst, there was someone who cared about you in spite of it all, someone who would not let you go, someone who was willing to make a fool of himself or herself if only it would help you. For many of us, this was our parents, but not for all of us; some of us will have had parents who failed us. Some of you will think of an aunt, a brother, a grandmother, a teacher, a youth leader, a spouse.

That person has conveyed to you a measure of the love of God in three persons. It is only a small measure, for the love of one human being for another is only a hint of the perfect love of God, but it is the most important hint that we have in this fallen world. Human love is a glimmer of the full radiance of God's love. As the Father loves the Son and the Son loves the Father and the Holy Spirit pours forth from that love, so God loves you.

And so today we offer worship and praise not to a vaguely imagined Something but to the Someone who is eternal and inexhaustible, yet personal, relational, and intimately loving, the God who pursues us even beyond the grave with his resurrection power. The God whom we adore on Trinity Sunday is the Three-Personed God whose own inner core of being is love, and whose nature it is to give that love to his creatures without restraint, without measure, without calculation, without ceasing.

This is no dry scholarly doctrine that we celebrate today. Nor is this a vague, romanticized version of human love. This is the love that upholds the universe, the love that has become incarnate in history through Jesus Christ, the love that persists in breaking through our resistance, the love that is with us even into the last ditch of our messed-up lives. And so I may leave you today with renewed confidence and trust in our God who is truly God, invoking with renewed faith the apostolic blessing, "The grace of the Lord Jesus Christ and the love of God and the fellowship of the Holy Spirit be with you all."

PRAYER

Almighty and everlasting God, who hast given unto us thy servants grace, by the confession of a true faith, to acknowledge the glory of the eternal Trinity, and in the power of thy Divine Majesty to worship the Unity: We beseech thee that thou wouldst keep us steadfast in this faith and worship, and bring us at last to see thee in thy one and eternal glory, O Father; who with the Son and the Holy Spirit livest and reignest, one God, for ever and ever. Amen.

Psalm 130

If you, O Lord, were to note what is done amiss,
Lord, who could stand?

—PSALM 130:3

The psalmist's cry above, from Psalm 130, is a very sweeping statement. There is no human being who can come up with enough credits to come into the presence of God as a righteous person.

There used to be a way of teaching all this from the Book of Common Prayer; in the version that we used until 1976, we said,

> We have erred and strayed like lost sheep. We have followed too much the devices and desires of our own hearts. We have offended against thy holy laws. We have left undone those things which we ought to have done, and we have done those things which we ought not to have done, and there is no health in us.

That statement, "there is no health in us," has been removed from the Episcopal prayer book that we now use. The removal of this line has robbed us of a powerful buttress to the biblical concept of sin as a "vast primordial catastrophe."[32] At the same time, the deletion has reduced the honor given to God's mercy, for "the less we deserve, the more merit is in his bounty."[33]

There was another phrase in the old prayer book that was removed. We used to describe ourselves in the General Confession as "miserable offenders." What was not removed, however, was the reading of this great psalm. It is called *De Profundis*, "out of the depths." It begins at rock bottom:

Out of the depths have I called to you, O Lord.

Over the centuries, these "depths" have been plumbed by countless sufferers who have cried out to God. This psalm has been recited by prisoners in solitary confinement, by the incurably ill, by victims of natural disasters, by those condemned to die, and in every other kind of distress and despair. Such use of the psalm has a long and honored history. However, the depth of which the psalmist is actually speaking here is the depth of the knowledge that he and everyone else is a "miserable offender."

If you, O Lord, were to note what is done amiss,
Lord, who could stand?

Biblical passages like these are the source of the statement "there is no health in us." The idea that we can add up our virtues and balance them over against our faults is decisively repudiated in this verse. Were we to add up all our merits in the sight of the one true God, our response would still be that of the tax collector in Jesus's story: "Lord, have mercy on me, a sinner" (Luke 18:13).

It seems that there are many who do not want to hear that we are "miserable offenders," and yet those who hear it and believe it find this confession to be the path of life. When we recognize that sin is not breaking rules but estrangement from the God in whom alone there is true redemption, then we are already beginning to move out of the realm of petty record keeping, of adding up points, onto the world stage where the "vast primordial catastrophe" is met by nothing less than the purpose of an all-powerful Father to redeem his entire creation from its impulse toward self-destruction.

This is the movement of Psalm 130, widely acknowledged to be one of the greatest of all the psalms. It begins in the depths with unflinching acknowledgment of the wretchedness of all humanity, our total inability to present ourselves righteous before the Lord. Precisely at the point of that confession, the psalmist is enabled to raise up his eyes in a startling shift of mood:

> Out of the depths have I called to you, O Lord....
> If you, O Lord, were to note what is done amiss,
>   Lord, who could stand?
> For there is forgiveness with you;
>   therefore you shall be feared. (130:1–4)

If we can only begin to understand what is meant here by the fear of the Lord, we will understand the one thing we really need to know in life and death. The fear of the Lord is the beginning of wisdom, as the Psalms and Proverbs repeatedly say. The fear of the Lord is founded on his absolute goodness. The fear of the Lord arises out of the discovery that he is a God of infinite mercy and compassion. Notice the surprising order of the words: "There is forgiveness with you; therefore you shall be feared." The forgiveness of sins does not leave us with a cheerful, domestic idea of God. Rather, it calls forth from us a new respect for the humanly incomprehensible majesty and greatness of the God who can redeem humanity from so grave a predicament.[34] ("The less we deserve, the more merit is in his bounty.") Our understanding of the incomparable glory of God will correspond to our sense of the depths of human pride, disobedience, perversity, and self-will.

It has been the experience of God's people down through the ages that deliverance and new life are to be found in the confession that before God there is something fundamentally, drastically, terribly wrong with all of us—not just the bigots and thugs, not just the pimps and the drug dealers, not just the Nazis and the goons of the gulags, but with all of us. Before God, none of us can hold up our heads. This is not self-abasement leading to paralysis; this is honesty leading to deliverance. Writes Samuel Terrien, "Not the man who is lost, but the man who is about to be saved can understand that he is a sinner."[35]

The psalm itself is a clear demonstration that the confession of sins before God is an entrance into a larger life. The psalmist ceases to reflect upon himself and his own problems, and in beautiful, ecstatic imagery, thinks of himself as a watchman on behalf of all the people, straining forward to the approach of the dawn.

May God grant that not a single one of us today would think himself too good to deserve any mercy, and that not a single one of us would think himself too bad to receive any mercy, and that we all together might go forth in the joyous and liberating knowledge that

> With the Lord there is mercy;
> with him there is plenteous redemption,
>   and he shall redeem Israel from all his iniquities.
>   (130:7–8)

PRAYER

Remember, O Lord, what thou hast wrought in us and not what we deserve; and, as thou hast called us to thy service, make us worthy of our calling; through Jesus Christ our Lord, who liveth and reigneth with thee and the Holy Spirit, one God, now and for ever. *Amen.*

THIRD SUNDAY AFTER PENTECOST

Romans 1:1–7

> Paul, a servant of Jesus Christ . . . through whom we [apostles] have received grace and apostleship to bring about the obedience of faith for the sake of his name.
>
> —ROMANS 1:1, 5

When Paul wrote his letter to the Christians in Rome, he introduced himself as "an apostle set apart for the gospel." It seems to me that when we think today of people who are set apart, we mean they have set themselves apart, like monks or nuns; or they are set apart because they have special skills or training. But this isn't at all what Paul meant when he said he had been set apart as an apostle for the gospel. He hadn't chosen this role; he was commandeered by the risen Christ on the road to Damascus. He didn't suit the role; on the contrary, as he himself wrote,

> I am the least of the apostles, unfit to be called an apostle, because I persecuted the church of God. But by the grace of God I am what I am, and his grace toward me was not in vain. (1 Cor. 15:9–10)

Let's remember: Saul of Tarsus, as he was then called, was an arrogant, self-righteous pharisaical type—indeed, he was the very thing itself, a Pharisee—who was fanatically committed to exterminating the new Christian faith. He was literally on the road, "breathing threats and murder against the disciples of the Lord," as the book of Acts says (Acts 9:1), aiming to do whatever was necessary to get rid of this heretical sect, when the Lord Jesus Christ knocked him off his horse and blinded him for three days. That was the moment of his calling, his set-apart-ness, to be an apostle, with credentials just as good as Peter's and John's even though he had never known Jesus personally. An apostle (Greek *apostolos*) was a disciple who had been promoted; a disciple is a follower, but an apostle is a fully commissioned ambassador. That is what God did with Paul. He took him from the camp of the enemy and sent him out to carry the gospel precisely to the people that Saul the Pharisee would have considered beneath him—namely, the ungodly gentiles.

So this man, this apostle Paul, risked life and limb a hundred times over as he traveled around the Mediterranean world in conditions so rugged that people today who try to trace his steps are amazed that he could do it. Add to that the fact that he was persecuted, imprisoned, and threatened with death almost everywhere he went, and you get some idea of how much we owe to the Lord's calling and commissioning of this apostle to the gentiles—that is, to us. Without Paul, there would have been no worldwide Christian faith. Most important to remember, it was not Paul by himself. It was, as he said repeatedly, "not I, but Christ in me."

At the beginning of Romans, let's recall that Paul is preparing for his biggest trip so far. He is coming to imperial Rome. We need to imagine the might of the Roman Empire compared to the infinitesimally small band of Christians there—the Colosseum looming over a handful of ants. Paul is determined to come in spite of the very real possibility that he will lose his life—as indeed he did. His letter is written to prepare the little congregation for his coming; many of them are personally named and greeted by Paul in the wonderful chapter 16. The central focus here is a phrase that Paul uses in his greeting to them: "the obedience of faith."

What exactly does that mean? "Obedience" is not in favor today. Contemporary culture prizes everything that is rebellious, edgy, transgressive. Staying within boundaries is nerdy; pushing the edge of the envelope is hip. It is disobedience that's in fashion, not obedience. It takes some effort to reappropriate obedience in the way that Paul means it. He, of course, means obedience to God. He returns to this theme at the end of his letter:

> I have written to you very boldly . . . because of the grace given me by God to be a minister . . . of the gospel of God, so that the offering of the Gentiles may be acceptable, sanctified by the Holy Spirit. . . . I will not venture to speak of anything except what Christ has wrought through me to win *obedience* from the Gentiles . . . by the power of the Holy Spirit. (Rom. 15:15–19)

To win obedience from the gentiles—that's you and me. Obedience by the power of the Holy Spirit. *The obedience of faith.* True freedom is not found in rebellion against God. Rebellion against God leads to the death of the soul and the spirit. Obedience to God may mean the death of the body, but it means life for the world.

When Paul speaks of the obedience of faith, it is not generic religion of which he speaks. He speaks of being "in Christ" (Rom. 8:1; 12:5; 16:9; etc.). He speaks of having "the mind of Christ" (1 Cor. 2:16; Phil. 2:5), "formation" in Christ (Gal. 4:19), being "in accord with Christ" (Rom. 15:5), "dying and rising" with Christ (Rom. 6:4–8; etc.). He speaks of "putting on the Lord Jesus Christ" (Rom. 13:14). He says we are letters from Christ to the world, "written not with ink but with the Spirit of the living God, not on tablets of stone but on tablets of human hearts" (2 Cor. 3:3). He even says that we are the fragrant aroma of Christ being spread by God throughout the world (2 Cor. 2:15). He says all these things so that we, those who are "baptized into Christ" (Rom. 6:3), would be a people prepared. This is the obedience of faith.

The obedience of faith in Jesus Christ does not mean restriction or claustrophobia or imprisonment. It means freedom. It means liberty. It means power. Karl Barth uses a phrase that caught my attention: "the power of obedience." Aligning oneself with the power of God in obedience to the Spirit: this is the power that overcomes the world.

PRAYER

O Almighty and most merciful God, of thy bountiful goodness keep us, we beseech thee, from all things that may hurt us, that we, being ready both in body and soul, may with free hearts accomplish those things which belong to thy purpose; through Jesus Christ our Lord, who liveth and reigneth with thee and the Holy Spirit, one God, now and for ever. *Amen.*

Genesis 22

"Take your son, your only son Isaac, whom you love, and go to the land of Moriah, and offer him there as a burnt offering upon one of the mountains of which I shall tell you."

—GENESIS 22:2

The story of Abraham's journey to sacrifice his son Isaac is well known, but it's necessary to see it in its total context. In Genesis 12, the Lord says to Abraham, "Leave your country, your people, and your father's house, and go to the land that I will show you" (12:1). This was no small thing to ask. It meant being severed from everything that made a man secure and consequential in those days. It meant abandoning every single anchor to the past and setting out in an unknown direction with nothing to trust except the Word of the Lord.

Abraham's life during the next decades was extremely difficult, for he had to live as a nomad in a foreign land. All those years, he and his wife, Sarah, had borne the sorrow of childlessness. Over and over and over, for a period of twenty-five years, God continued to appear to Abraham and make promises.

How hollow, how false God's promise must have seemed, when Abraham and Sarah were both approaching their hundredth year and Sarah had never once conceived in her whole life! But, as Saint Paul says, Abraham went on hoping against hope because of the God in whom he believed, the God who calls into existence the things that do not exist (Rom. 4:19–21).

Finally, in their extreme old age, Sarah conceived and bore Abraham a son, Isaac—the child of the promise. A lifetime of obedience had been rewarded; Abraham had remained faithful; at length, God had kept his word.

Then the unthinkable happens.

This last climactic story of Abraham is told in the same form as the first:

Leave your country,	Take your son,
your people,	your only son Isaac,
and your father's house	whom you love,
and go to the land	and go to one of the mountains
that I will show you (12:1).	that I will tell you about (22:2).

In chapter 12, Abraham is asked to cut himself off from the past; in chapter 22, he is asked to cut himself off from the future.[36]

What sort of God would do such a thing? That is the question we ask. But apparently, according to the story, the answer to the question is that it is the same God that Abraham has known and believed and obeyed from the beginning. This seems incredible to us, but it is a feature of the story that Abraham seems to believe that God is entirely within his rights to demand this of him.

The most dreadful part of the story, of course, is that Abraham is supposed to do the deed himself—and first has to take a three-day journey to do it. Three days! Conceivably one might carry out an unthinkable order on impulse, in a moment's blind recklessness; but God sends Abraham to a distant spot so that he will have plenty of time to think about what he has been asked to do.

Is this some kind of cruel joke? God already knows everything; why then does he put Abraham to the test? A clue is found in Romans when Paul calls Abraham "the father of us all." It is Abraham's faith, the meaning of it, the depth of it, the application of it, and above all, the *source* of it, that is central to the story of the sacrifice of Isaac.

Abraham was asked to do something that no one else was ever asked to do, precisely in order to demonstrate to the whole world what hope in God really means. We look upon Abraham's three-day journey with solemn awe. We are amazed by his faith in the God whose promise he had trusted for decades, his obedience to the God with whom he had walked—the God whose gifts and promises are manifestations of pure grace, to be received from his hand in total submission to the one whose will, whether in light or in shadow, is always perfect.

And at the very moment that we avert our eyes in unspeakable horror, God acts. Abraham receives his son back from the dead. To "believe in" God, to "fear" God, is to trust him totally and to put oneself in his hands totally, even when the road leads out into God-forsakenness, even when the fulfillment of God's promises seems to have receded into impossibility. Our father Abraham, through his three days' agony, has taught us how to be believers.

God knew that Abraham would be faithful; the purpose of the "test" was not for God to gain new knowledge but for Abraham to bequeath to his posterity a heroic, unparalleled example of steadfast loyalty to God throughout a journey into an apparently hopeless night.

Unparalleled, that is, until the day when God's own Son, his only Son, whom God loved, cried out on the cross, "My God, my God, why hast thou forsaken me?" For Isaac, there was a substitute—Abraham found a ram in the bush. "God himself will provide the lamb for a burnt offering, my son." But when Jesus was brought to the cross—the Lamb of God who would bear the sin of the world into fathomless darkness—there was no substitute for him. God did not withhold his Son, his only Son, whom he loved.

God the Father and God the Son together, with a single will, offered the perfect sacrifice once for all. What Abraham at the last moment did not have to do, God did.

And what this means for you and for me is that there is nothing so unspeakable that God has not already thought of it, and nothing so evil that God is not victorious over it, however long the journey may be, however indefinitely the fulfillment of the promises may seem to be postponed. What this means is that you and I, as children of Abraham, Isaac, and Jacob, have received our lives from God as pure gift, sustained in his hand, according to his purpose, destined for the completion of his plan, living solely by his grace. In the life of faith lived by Christians, we bear witness to the biblical testimony that nothing—nothing at all—can destroy the promised future, because the promised future belongs to our God.

PRAYER

Grant, O Lord, we beseech thee, that the course of this world may be peaceably governed by thy providence; and that thy Church may joyfully serve thee in confidence and serenity; through Jesus Christ our Lord, who liveth and reigneth with thee and the Holy Spirit, one God, for ever and ever. *Amen.*

John 6:22–71

Simon Peter answered him, "Lord, to whom shall we go? You have the words of eternal life; and we have believed, and have come to know, that you are the Holy One of God."

—JOHN 6:68–69

S ome years ago my husband and I were spending the weekend at a summer colony where the summer chapel service was always packed. Many people attended the summer chapel who never went to church anywhere else. At a dinner party the conversation turned to this subject. One couple said that, for them, the summer chapel service was a social occasion and a time for the lusty singing of hymns, but that they weren't believers in any sense of the word. Why not? I inquired. "Because," said the wife, firmly and decisively, "I don't need it."

I thought about that later when the news came of a fiery airplane crash. I heard the president say on the radio that we could not get through such terrible times without faith in God. I wondered about that. There is always a suspicion about religion, that it is just made up by us in order to make an unbearable situation bearable. If this is true, then the person who says she doesn't need religion is more honest, more courageous, more sophisticated than the rest of us weak and benighted souls. Clearly, that is what the woman at the dinner party thought.

A long line of Christian theologians and biblical scholars

insists that the Judeo-Christian tradition is *not religion*. The dictionary gives a number of definitions of religion, all of them originating as human activities: worship, belief, ritual. We are so used to thinking of religion that way, whether we are believers or not, that it comes as quite a shock to discover from the Scriptures of the Old and New Testaments, from the Hebrew prophets to the apostle Paul, that *God is not interested in religion*. Religion is a human construct, allowing people to create a God after their own image instead of the other way round. Religion makes God more manageable by setting up conditions that God will be bound by. If God is a construction of our own, then we are indeed deceived and the whole biblical enterprise is false.

In the Gospel of John, there is a moment in the ministry of Jesus when a number of his disciples turn away from him. Early in his ministry, Jesus had more disciples than he did at the end. His huge popular following did not stay the course, because he did not fit the people's idea of what the Messiah should be. This turning away begins at the end of the sixth chapter, after the great discourse on the Bread of Life. The religious authorities take offense at him. Jesus's claim to be "from heaven" is shocking to those who know that he is just a local boy, but worse still, he identifies himself as the one who reveals God.

Here is the crucial distinction between "religion" and the confession of Jesus Christ; he is not the fulfillment of human wishes, but the one who reveals a God whom none of us could ever have imagined. In the evangelist's words in the preface, we hear once again the teaching of the Old Testament that God is inaccessible to human religious aspiration: "No one has ever seen God." Then John announces the unique revelation of "the only Son, who is in the bosom of the Father, he has made him known" (1:18). This has never been an easy message to assimilate.

Jesus becomes even more specific, and now he angers not

only the pooh-bahs but his own disciples: "'The one who eats my flesh and drinks my blood abides in me, and I in him.... This is the bread which came down from heaven ... he who eats this bread will live for ever.' This he said in the synagogue, as he taught at Capernaum. Many of his disciples, when they heard it, said, 'This is a hard saying; who can listen to it?'" (John 6:56-60). It can't be said too often: the *specificity* of Jesus, the "scandal of particularity" as it is called, goes against the grain of ordinary religiosity. Not only do the leaders react against this concreteness, many of Jesus's own disciples react against it too. And so we read, "After this many of his disciples drew back and no longer went about with him. Jesus said to the twelve, 'Do you also wish to go away?' Simon Peter answered him, 'Lord, to whom shall we go? You have the words of eternal life; and we have believed, and have come to know, that you are the Holy One of God'" (6:66-69).

I have often thought about that woman at the dinner party, and many other people I know. If it is "religion" that she doesn't need, then she is in good company with the Hebrew prophets. But if it is the Lord Jesus Christ and his words of eternal life that she is rejecting, then that is a different matter.

Why do terrible things happen? I do not know. Have I any proof that what the church proclaims is true? Only the faith of those who have put their trust in Jesus as the Son of God. Is this wishful thinking? Maybe. I do not believe so. With all due respect to the religions of the world, there is no other story like the Christian story. Today's passage means a great deal to me. I cannot count the number of times that I, too, have felt like drawing back from the stance of faith because horrible things happen and I just don't see any evidence that the Christian promises are true. But then I hear the Lord saying to me, "Do you also wish to go away?" and I find myself answering with Peter, "Lord, to whom shall we go? You have the words of eternal life; and we have believed, and have come to know, that you are the Holy One of God."

The eternal God who created the heavens and the earth has come down from his throne on high into his creation and has submitted to the fury of its rebellion and wickedness by his own free will in order to deliver us from everlasting sin and death. There is no other story like this. We do not proclaim "religion" today. We come together to hear the living voice of a living Lord, who has passed through the domain of death and hell and emerged victorious, bearing the keys with him. He has the words of eternal life. May we all today put our trust in him, as we come to know that he is the Holy One of God.

PRAYER

O God, whose never-failing providence ordereth all things both in heaven and earth: We humbly beseech thee to put away from us all hurtful things, and give us those things which are profitable for us; through Jesus Christ our Lord, who liveth and reigneth with thee and the Holy Spirit, one God, for ever and ever. *Amen.*

Psalm 145; Deuteronomy 26:6–11

> One generation shall laud thy works to another,
> and shall declare thy mighty acts.

—PSALM 145:4

What are the wonderful deeds of God? If you look at Psalm 78, you will see that it is a long recitation of the mighty acts of God. It goes on for seventy-two verses. The children of Israel in the psalmist's time, and in Jesus's time, could say all of this by heart. Psalm 105 is another psalm in two parts that recounts the wonderful works of God. In Psalm 106 you will see the same pattern. There are many shorter versions of the history of God's mighty acts, too. The most important one is in our reading today from Deuteronomy.

Every child of the covenant was brought up knowing this history of the mighty acts of God, and we may be sure that our Lord learned this at his mother's knee. But now we must acknowledge that we, today, children of a somewhat confused American culture, are distanced from these great biblical history lessons. What, exactly, is a mighty act of God? The discernment of such acts is a task of the Christian community.

Here is a real-life example. Let us imagine ourselves back in Birmingham, Alabama, in May of 1963. Many of us white folks did not recognize it at the time—our discernment was faulty—but one of the great struggles of human history was in progress. All across the South, but especially in Birmingham that month, ordinary black working people were acting out of a courage and resolve that most of us today can scarcely imagine. Police dogs and fire hoses were the least of the dangers; beatings, jail sentences, even death were more tolerable than the ever-present likelihood of being simply ignored and forgotten in the eyes of a nation far more interested in uncovering nonexistent communist conspiracies than in the struggles of black people to sit at lunch counters. Remember, this is before the March on Washington: the civil rights movement had not yet entered history. Virtually no white person had ever heard Martin Luther King speak. Most of us—I include myself as first in that line—most of us white Southerners who lived through that time missed the moment of destiny because we did not discern what was happening.

During the struggle in cities across the South, the civil rights warriors were sustained by the regular mass meetings in the churches—which were really worship services as well as rallies. Jackie Robinson spoke at one of the meetings at historic Sixteenth Street Baptist Church. I have not heard the tape of this meeting myself, but J. Louis Martyn describes it this way:

> He begins his speech by remarking, "You people are doing a great thing here in Birmingham." At this, one hears a few feet shuffling back and forth. After three or four sentences he says again, "It is a great thing you people are doing here." Shufflings of the feet, to which is added a few clearings of the throat. Several sentences later, he returns to what is now obviously his theme: "... You are doing a great thing here in Birmingham." Now shuffling of the feet and clearing of the throat will no longer suffice. One of the old deacons interrupts the speaker, politely but firmly, by calling out *"We are not doing this! God is doing this!"*[37]

How can we discern the mighty acts of God? What movement of his Spirit is God calling you to join? It may not be a great and glorious world-historical struggle. It may only be a seemingly small and insignificant skirmish, but nevertheless part of God's great plan. Where, today, is God bringing us "out of Egypt with a mighty hand and an outstretched arm"? What Red Seas are being crossed? How is God leading his people out of bondage into freedom? Where is he leading us "out of error into truth, out of sin into righteousness, out of death into life"?[38] What unmerited suffering can you contribute to God's great purpose for human liberation?

This discernment of God's purpose will be for you to discover. What I hope to do for you here is to remind you to discern when it is time to shuffle your feet. What I hope to do is to encourage you to know when it is time to clear your throat. And sometimes you might need to remind yourself, "We're not doing this! God is doing this!" Because as soon as you get the idea that you are doing it, you will be back in the house of bondage again—the bondage of spiritual blindness, the bondage of moral arrogance, the bondage of self-righteousness that is not able to embrace the brother or sister on the other side of the issue.

In Ephesians we read, "By grace you have been saved through faith; and this is not your own doing, it is the gift of God—and not because of works, lest any one should boast" (Eph. 2:8–9).

It is not your doing; it is the gift of God. What, then, is the place of human action? If God is doing everything, what is there for us to do? We read on in the passage: "For we are God's workmanship, created in Christ Jesus for good works, which God prepared beforehand, that we should walk in them" (2:10).

It is by God's grace that we do the good works. God is doing this, but human beings are the agents. We are not doing this; God is doing this. And yet, wonder of wonders, he is doing it through us, through you—flawed, yes; sinful, yes; unworthy, yes; but beloved of God and chosen to act for him in the great battle against oppression, sin, and death in which you are the Christian soldiers.

Hear the word of the Lord:

The Lord heard your voice, and saw your affliction … and the Lord brought you out of [your bondage] with a mighty hand and with an outstretched arm.

Praised be his holy Name! Now his arm is stretched out through you toward others. Now he is preparing all those good works for you to walk in. This is the freedom train—not just the freedom of those to whom we minister, but your freedom, our freedom. Our God is on the move. You don't want to miss your moment with destiny. The fare has already been paid. The Lord is on a roll. The kingdom of heaven is at hand.

Just remember: You are not doing this. God is doing this.

PRAYER

O God, from whom all good doth come: Grant that by thy inspiration we may think those things that are right, and by thy merciful guiding may perform the same; through Jesus Christ our Lord, who liveth and reigneth with thee and the Holy Spirit, one God, for ever and ever. *Amen.*

Ecclesiastes; 1 Samuel 16:7

Man looks on the outward appearance, but the Lord looks on the heart.

—1 SAMUEL 16:7

I t is well known that Americans are optimistic and upbeat. "Positive thinking" is one of our cultural traits. We don't always recognize that people in other parts of the world are not like us. The market for "motivational" and "inspirational" speakers is not as lively in other parts of the world as it is here.

The book of Ecclesiastes is a very important book of the Old Testament. It would be a good thing for our relentlessly optimistic, upbeat Western form of Christianity if we all read Ecclesiastes regularly. Everybody knows the part about "a time to live and a time to die," but that's the least of the book. The person who wrote it (traditionally Solomon, but we don't really know who) was a realist about human life. No pieties for him, no denial, no making nice, no pretense that everything is working out fine. Judy Collins never sang this part of Ecclesiastes:

> This is an evil in all that is done under the sun, that one fate comes to all; also the hearts of men are full of evil, and madness is in their hearts while they live, and after that they go to the dead. (9:3)

Qoheleth would not be at all surprised to see the president of the company laid low by ALS (amyotrophic lateral sclerosis), or depression, or personal tragedy, or failure of any kind. Not even human wisdom works as a bulwark against the whims of a world threatened by meaninglessness:

> One fate comes to all, to the righteous and the wicked.... The race is not to the swift, nor the battle to the strong, neither yet bread to the wise, nor yet riches to men of understanding, nor yet favor to men of skill; but time and chance happeneth to them all. (9:2, 11)

This is what Qoheleth sees. What does God see when he looks at us? He sees us running around after success and status and sex and eternal youth, and it is all "striving after wind," in the repeated refrain of Ecclesiastes: "this also is vanity and a striving after wind."

Moreover, in the tradition of the Hebrew prophets, Qoheleth goes on to say that heedlessness does not excuse us from participating in a system that elevates the rich and neglects the poor. The judgment of God lies upon such a society:

> In the place of justice, even there was wickedness.... Behold, the tears of the oppressed, and they had no one to comfort them! On the side of their oppressors there was power, and there was no one to comfort them. (3:16; 4:1)

I wonder if you've had the experience of visiting a socially prominent friend in the hospital. It can be a startling experience. You're used to seeing this person working the crowds, looming over others by force of personality, cutting a figure, working his or her will. Suddenly there the person is, lying prone on a bed in a hospital gown, pale, hair messed up, arms and throat vulnerably exposed, attached to tubes, perhaps, with a facial expression of discomfort and embarrassment, if not fear.

Ecclesiastes plays a very important role in Scripture. It asks us to see through the images that we invent for ourselves:

images of power and prosperity, youth and beauty, vigor and health, energy and significance. It asks us—indeed, it forces us—to see that we are more like patients in a hospital than masters of the universe. Which is the real person? Is it the person who is up and moving, dressed in a power suit, impressing people, totally in command? Or is it the frightened, defenseless person in the bed?

Well, the answer to that, humanly speaking, is of course both; but there can be no question as to how God sees us. "Almighty God, unto whom all hearts are open, all desires known, and from whom no secrets are hid"[39]—our Father in heaven sees us in the full dimensions of our weakness and mortality, without pretenses, without defenses; and he loves us.

What does God see when he sees the man in the bed, the woman in the ICU? He sees a person that he loves. He sees a person that he loves more than life, more than glory, more than power, more than riches, more than divinity itself:

> For you know the grace of our Lord Jesus Christ, who though he was rich, yet for your sake he became poor, so that by his poverty you might become rich. (2 Cor. 8:9)

> Christ Jesus was in the form of God, but he did not think equality with God a thing to be grasped, but emptied himself, taking the form of a slave ... becoming obedient unto death, even to death on a cross. (Phil. 2:6–8)

And why did he do that?

Because he loved you. Because he loved me. He looked at us and saw our pretensions and our delusions and our false fronts and our sickness unto death, and he loved us. "God shows his love for us in that while we were still sinners, Christ died for us" (Rom. 5:8). What is Jesus doing on that cross? Is it "negative"? Is it frightening? Is it horrifying? Is it ugly? Yes, it is all of those things, but is it not also the greatest story ever told?

Here is the news from the cross of Christ. The one and only Master of the universe, the Lord who created the cosmos with his mere word, the almighty and omnipotent Holy One of Israel, the God who parted the Red Sea and caused the walls of Jericho to fall and answered Elijah on Mount Carmel with a bolt of lightning has entered human flesh and laid himself down on our hospital bed. The Son of God has exposed his throat, his arms, his entire body to the scorn and abuse of the multitude. He has taken ultimate shame and weakness upon himself. These are the glad words from the First Epistle of Peter:

> He himself bore our sins in his body on the tree, that we might die to sin and live to righteousness. By his wounds you have been healed. For you were straying like sheep, but now you have returned to the Shepherd and Guardian of your souls. (1 Pet. 2:24–25)

PRAYER

Keep, O Lord, we beseech thee, thy household the Church in thy steadfast faith and love, that by the help of thy grace we may proclaim thy truth with boldness, and minister thy justice with compassion; for the sake of our Savior Jesus Christ, who liveth and reigneth with thee and the Holy Spirit, one God, now and for ever. *Amen.*

EIGHTH SUNDAY AFTER PENTECOST

Genesis 15

When the sun had gone down and it was dark, behold, a smoking fire pot and a flaming torch passed between these pieces.

—GENESIS 15:17

G enesis 15 is one of the most remarkable passages in the Old Testament. At the beginning we discover Abraham in his tent at night, a very old man with an elderly, barren wife and not a single legitimate child. He has been trekking through the Near East for decades, trusting in a promise for which there was no evidence whatsoever. We can hardly blame Abraham for complaining to God that he was having a hard time trying to believe that he was going to have an heir who would be a blessing to all the nations of the earth. God is patient with Abraham's skepticism; he leads the old man out into the desert night and says, "Look toward heaven, and count the stars, if you are able. So shall your descendants be."

Now we come to the eerie part of the story. When it is still daylight, God instructs Abraham to bring three animals and two birds. Abraham slaughters them according to the ritual traditions of that primitive time. Then he cuts each animal and bird in half, and lays out the pieces in two rows, with an alley between the halves.

This ritual was the first step in a very ancient covenant-making ceremony. After the carcasses were laid out, the second step constituted the two covenant partners passing through the bloody passageway as a sign of solemn commitment to one another. The point was that, if either partner violated the terms of the covenant, he was leaving himself open to suffering the fate of the slaughtered animals.

Abraham did all the things he was told to do, and then, not knowing what would come next, he waited. Buzzards began to come down to eat the carcasses, and Abraham kept busy driving them away. As evening draws near and darkness begins to fall over the strange scene, the biblical narrator begins to cast his spell with the extraordinary economy and narrative skill for which Old Testament storytelling is admired. "As the sun was going down," we read, "a deep sleep fell on Abram, and lo, a dread and great darkness fell upon him." That is all we are told of Abraham's state of mind; the psychological details that interest modern people are omitted. All the emphasis is on the solemnity of the event that is about to occur, the action of God.

Now, recall the purpose of the bloody passageway. If the two partners making the covenant are equals, they will each pass through. That will be a sign from one to the other, both of them, that they intend to keep their covenant or else call down a curse upon themselves. However, if one partner greatly outranks the other, then only the weaker partner would be required to pass through. The suspense in the story is built up with utmost simplicity, but it's palpable; the atmosphere as night falls over the bloody alley is heavy with foreboding. Human activity, human wishing, human willing has come to an end; indeed, the human agent has fallen asleep. The only actor remaining on the stage is God.

And then, in the darkness, Abraham awakens from his premonitory sleep, and he sees a smoking firepot and a flaming torch move through the aisle of blood. It is the living presence of God.

In that ceremony, we read, God made a covenant with Abraham. The Creator of the universe has come down into the hu-

man story and has bound himself in blood to his mortal creatures. But do you get the amazing revelation here, the missing
piece that means everything? God passes through the bloody
alley. Abraham does not. The Lord alone passes through, acting
in the role of the weaker party. In this extraordinary event, God
attaches himself unconditionally to his fallen human creatures
and ratifies his commitment unilaterally.

There is nothing else like this in the history of religion: the
almighty Lord of the universe enters into a relationship with
his chosen human partner under the conditions of human
liability. Here in the opening pages of the story of salvation,
God lays himself open to the full consequences of everything
that will come after: the disobedience, the idolatry, the folly,
the greed and cruelty, the vanity and selfishness, the pride and
deceit that fill the following pages of the Bible.

You know how the story continues with the birth of Abraham and Sarah's son, Isaac, and how it comes to its appointed
culmination two thousand years later, when God keeps his
word and takes the bloody curse upon himself. After the people
of God have flagrantly disregarded their part in the covenant
for thousands of years, God at last steps forward and, on a hill
outside Jerusalem, ratifies the covenant for once and for all in
the blood of his Son. The fiery presence of Yahweh in the midnight spectacle of the bloody alley becomes the pouring out of
the last drop of blood of the Son of God.

Every single one of us today, no matter how prosperous and
glossy we may look, is carrying some sort of baggage. Human
life is a bloody affair. If it is not the blood of war and murder,
it is the blood of illness and death. If it is not literally blood, it
is the burden of disappointment, doubt, anxiety, depression,
fear.

We are all terminally afflicted with the human condition,
incapable of making or keeping any kind of agreement with a
righteous God. Here is the news today: it is precisely to us in
our affliction that the Lord comes, blazing his way with gal-

axies across the sky, trailing clouds of glory, writing his name in fire. He comes to us in our insensibility, in our stupor, in our impotence. He comes without conditions and without requirements. He comes down from heaven into the bloody mess of human history, laying himself open to the worst that we can do, taking the curse of our condition upon himself. He takes it and he carries it all the way.

This is the God of Abraham, Isaac, and Jacob; this is the God and Father of our Lord Jesus Christ. Let him take you by the hand this very day and lead you out where you can see the stars, where the flaming splendor of his appearance dispels your darkness, and above all, where he lays himself down in the corridors of death, so that the children of Abraham might, by his blood, attain to the promise of eternal life and a celestial inheritance in the kingdom that fadeth not away.

PRAYER

O Lord, we beseech thee, make us to have a perpetual fear and love of thy holy Name, for thou never failest to help and govern those whom thou hast set upon the sure foundation of thy loving-kindness; through Jesus Christ our Lord, who liveth and reigneth with thee and the Holy Spirit, one God, for ever and ever. *Amen.*

NINTH SUNDAY AFTER PENTECOST

Romans 6:1–14

For if we have been united with him in a death like his, we shall certainly be united with him in a resurrection like his.

—ROMANS 6:5

When I write sermons about Sin and Death, I capitalize those two words. The purpose of doing this is to show that Sin and Death are not just components of human life, but Powers that rule over us. That is the way Paul understands the situation. In our text for today he uses words that indicate their sovereign sway. Sin *reigns*, he says; Death *has dominion*; we are *enslaved by* Sin. Sin is not something we can choose to avoid, any more than we can choose not to die.

In Romans 6 Paul leaves behind the long descriptions of how we have fallen into the grip of Sin, and he launches into a kind of rhapsody about what happens to Christians when we are baptized. His teaching here is so audacious and original that I am swept away by it every time I preach from it. Paul says that those who are baptized into Christ are crucified with Christ, meaning that all the benefits of his death become ours. He says that our sinful selves are put to death on the cross so that we are no longer slaves to Sin.

In baptism the Holy Spirit acts to unite the person to Christ in his death and therefore to the death of the sinful self. All the things we find upsetting about ourselves, the habits we cannot seem to shake, the personality traits that get us in trouble,

the secret obsessions and perversions that we struggle to hide
even from ourselves—all of this has been put to death.

Paul knew that there was a danger in this teaching. We are
frightened to death of the message of God's grace. In order to
understand this fright, we need to go back a bit in Romans. In
the section just before this one, Paul explains that "Christ's
act of righteousness [on the cross] leads to acquittal and life
for all human beings" (5:18); and then he says the even more
dangerous thing: "Where sin increased, grace abounded all
the more" (5:20). Paul knew that some people would misunderstand this and say, "Wow! If grace abounds all the more
when sin increases, bring it on! Let's sin all the more!" But
this is indeed to misunderstand totally, as Paul says in our
text today: "Are we to continue in sin that grace may abound?
By no means!"

I've been trying to think of a way to put this across. If you've
been living in a prison and are set free, would you want to go
back to it? If you conquer a bad habit, would you want to take
it up again? But that doesn't really work, does it? It is well
known; we *do* go back to bad habits, more often than not. The
fact that this is so is evidence of the power of Sin, which "reigns
in death" (Rom. 5:21).

What are we to make of the fact that we slip back into Sin
so frequently? We do that, Paul seems to be saying, but Sin no
longer determines us. It no longer rules our lives in the same
total way. In our baptisms something objective has happened,
something that comes to us from outside ourselves, and as we
grow into the baptismal life, we more and more recognize how
we can appropriate this great truth:

For if we have been united with him in a death like his, we
shall certainly be united with him in a resurrection like his.

Union with Christ! United with him in his death, united
with him in the resurrection of the dead. In other religious

systems, in Gnostic systems, the religious elite are supposed to do this for themselves. We seek after union with the divine, and if we get it right, we find enlightenment, or the higher consciousness, or some other sort of oneness with the divine. The Christian story is the opposite of this. We could do nothing for ourselves, religiously or otherwise, because the iron grip of Sin and Death separated us from God by such a chasm that there was no hope for us. God bridged that gap in his own person. It is in our new identity with him that we find our future. This news is so incomparable that Paul is seized by its joy.

So this unity with our Lord Jesus is something that exists in real lives and cannot be defeated by Sin. Our union with him is something that God has done, and therefore there is nothing we can do to undo it, because he is stronger than Sin, stronger than Death. He has shown this in the resurrection of Christ from the dead.

This breathtaking declaration of deliverance for us makes all the difference in the world. Indeed, it is a new world, not anything like the old one. We have a new power over Sin now. We can live as new people. That's what Paul means when he says, By no means! You aren't going to sin more so that grace may abound; "How can we who died to sin still live in it?" (6:2).

Perhaps you have heard that Paul's ethical teaching can be summarized in these words: "Become what you already are!" You already are an instrument of God's righteousness because he has made you that way, by uniting you with Christ in your baptism. Now you can actually be an instrument of God's righteousness! You can act like one! What liberation!

There is a paradox here, however, that nothing I can say will remove in this life. The paradox must remain until the last day. In this life we remain, as Martin Luther put it, saints and sinners simultaneously (simul iustus et peccator). We are sinners, but everything has changed because we are now justified sinners. We are sinners not only declared righteous but actually on our way to being made righteous. Only God can do this work. He has already done it, in the death and resurrection of Christ. We are assimilated into his cross, into his risen life.

The death and resurrection of Christ was not something that was over and done with long ago. It is present in all its majestic force right now, for the Word of God is living and active, creating new lives and new hope and new victories wherever it is heard.

PRAYER

O Lord, we beseech thee mercifully to receive the prayers of thy people who call upon thee, and grant that they may both perceive and know what things they ought to do, and also may have grace and power faithfully to fulfill the same; through Jesus Christ our Lord, who liveth and reigneth with thee and the Holy Spirit, one God, now and for ever. *Amen.*

Genesis 2–3

The Lord God called to the man, and said to him, "Where are you?"

—GENESIS 3:9

The Bible begins with the world created by God; chapter I ends this way: "and God saw everything that he had made, and behold, it was very good." By chapter II, at the end of the primeval history, we have seen fratricide, corruption, flood, arrogance, greed, lying, strife, and violence. What happened? What went wrong?

The garden that God planted for man and woman to live in was perfection. It was, in a word, paradise. Maybe we have a hard time even understanding what paradise is. The garden of Eden does not depict a bower of sensual delight like some depictions of paradise but, rather, a life of free obedience in the service and in the care of God.[40] Whatever paradise may have been like, I know it was not like my life. Maybe that is the only way we know to imagine it, in negatives—in paradise, no labor would be in vain, no thieves would break in and steal, no love would be rejected, no one would come to harm, there would be no discrepancy between my needs and my world.

There was only one limitation for Adam and Eve. They were not to eat of the tree of the knowledge of good and evil. Knowledge, biblically speaking, means "experience." The first couple were not created to experience evil. They were in a state of innocent ignorance. There is no suggestion in the story that it even occurs to them to eat the fruit from the forbidden tree until suddenly there is an idea presented from outside, from the snake. "Did God say 'You shall not eat of the fruit'?" (3:1). The seeds of doubt are sown. For the first time, the thought occurs: Perhaps the command is unreasonable. Perhaps God, the one giving the command, is not entirely trustworthy.

Eve is attracted by the serpent's clever arguments. How familiar they are! How many times we have heard them and heeded them! "It won't hurt you; you don't know what you've been missing." Eve thinks it over. She "saw that it was good for food; it was a delight to the eyes; it was to be desired to make one wise." She is far more energetic and imaginative here than her husband: she eats the fruit because she is drawn by the snake's clever rhetoric. Adam, on the other hand, just goes compliantly along: "She gave some to her husband, and he ate" (3:6).

The effects are instantaneous: shame and fear. Uneasy self-consciousness comes in where before there had been no thought of self at all. How do I look? What will he think? What will she think? We can't let God see us like this!

First, shame; then, fear. The relationship with the Creator has been totally disrupted. Until the disobedience, the thought of hiding from God would have been inconceivable; there was no reason, no need to hide. We need to let this sink in; the posture of hiding is pathetic, ludicrous. There they are, Adam and Eve—our primal ancestors and representatives, hiding in the bushes, feeling like craven fools and scared almost literally to death—death, which they had not known before. They are no longer innocent, no longer ignorant—now they have experience of evil as well as good. In a sense they are wiser, yes, but at the cost of unleashing evil upon the entire created order, from the lowest to the highest.

This is our condition. The choices that Adam and Eve had are no longer open to us. There is no going back. Fear and shame are our chronic symptoms. We are, so to speak, in the bushes for good, hoping that God will not find us. We are so far gone from original righteousness that we don't even realize we are subject to fear and shame because we have neglected his righteous commandments, which are for our good, for our safety, for our happiness. We are hiding wherever we can find the nearest cover—hiding in our offices, hiding in alcohol, hiding in busyness, hiding in affluence, hiding in self-deception. And this is what we hear God say: "Adam, where are you?" Fill in your name. Tom, Dick, Harry, Mary, Jane, Ann—where are you?

What is the answer to this question? Where are you in relation to God? Where are you in relation to others? Where are you in relation to the person God created you to be? Where are we? In the terms of the story, the way it is told throughout the Bible, there can be only one answer: We are lost. We may not think we are lost; we may have convinced ourselves that we have everything figured out. But when God puts the question to us, our human pretense at knowing all the answers evaporates.

"Man's first disobedience": this is what went wrong with the creation. The breach in creation, the fissure between God's rule and the rule of Sin and Death, occurred because the human race, including you and me as descendants of Adam and Eve, became rebellious and disobedient to the core—idolatrous, faithless, selfish. There is a distinct suggestion that humanity is not the origin of evil; rather, humanity capitulates to the evil that is already there, and in doing so, "lets hell loose."[41]

What the origin of evil is we cannot say. The Bible is silent. What we can say for certain is that God is in control of it. He puts the snake in its place immediately—on its belly in the dust. As for Adam and Eve, their marital harmony is miserably disrupted: Eve's desire for her husband will result in the multiplication of labor pains, and he will dominate her with previously unintended oppressiveness. Adam's work will no longer be a joy, and it will be an endless labor to make it productive; the ground will produce thorns and thistles. "Adam, where are you?" Lost, lost—and the world lost, too.

And yet . . . and yet. This is the God who comes seeking his lost creation. It can't be said often enough: the Bible is not the story of the human search for God; it is the story of the divine search for us. Here it is, right here in the third chapter of Genesis. This is the God who comes to man and woman when we can no longer come to him, when we can only run away and hide. "Adam, where are you?" This is the first thing that happens from God's side. Hardly a minute elapses between the catastrophic fall and the action of God, who comes seeking his lost children.

PRAYER

Almighty God, the fountain of all wisdom, who knowest our necessities before we ask and our ignorance in asking: Have compassion, we beseech thee, upon our infirmities, and those things which for our unworthiness we dare not, and for our blindness we cannot ask, mercifully give us for the worthiness of thy Son Jesus Christ our Lord, who liveth and reigneth with thee and the Holy Spirit, one God, now and for ever. *Amen.*

Romans 8

It is God who justifies; who is to condemn?

—ROMANS 8:33–34

The best-known passage in Paul's letter to the Romans is almost certainly chapter 8. The last part of it is often read at funerals. Because of that, American Christians generally think of this passage as a promise made to individuals at the time of death, or in time of personal trouble. That is certainly not wrong, but hearing it exclusively in this way prevents us from understanding the full gospel that Paul proclaims.

To do that, we have to go back to the early chapters of this letter to the Christians in Rome. Paul writes extended passages about a threat to humanity far greater than the death of individual persons. Indeed, he is writing on a cosmic scale. In the first chapters he writes about the wrath of God against the universal disobedience of the entire human race. When he gets to chapter 8, he enlarges this; he writes of the whole creation having been "subjected to futility." He says the entire cosmos is "in bondage to decay." He has the whole of human history and all of the created universe in view. When he speaks of angels, principalities, and powers, he is thinking of forces, beings, systems, and structures that were created by God for his good purposes but are now fallen from their place and actively opposed to God. Humanity is enslaved by these principalities and powers, but Paul declares that none of them can separate us from the love of God in Christ Jesus our Lord.

What we have trouble understanding in our culture today is that the only thing we had any right to expect was rejection by God. We don't grasp this because we live in a religious atmosphere that speaks exclusively of God's love, never of God's judgment. We hear a hundred variations of the message that God includes everybody, embraces everybody, accepts everybody just as they are. The idea that there is *something seriously wrong with all human beings* is not part of the church's message these days. Yet a fundamental presupposition of Paul's gospel message is the fact that, as he writes in chapter 3, "There is no one righteous, no, not one.... For there is no distinction; since all have sinned and fall short of the glory of God." Nothing Paul says in Romans can be understood apart from that diagnosis of the human condition.

This is the context for Paul's extraordinary promise at the end of Romans 8. When he asks, "Who will separate us from the love of Christ?" he isn't just thinking of death with a small d. He is thinking of Death as an annihilating Power that rules over us even now, in life, with Sin as its sinister cohort. He means the whole complex of forces that throw humanity off course, that pervert our best instincts and distort our best efforts. He means the consequences of disobedience, the result of rebellion against the purposes of God—in other words, the judgment of God. And as he has already made clear, that judgment was due to every human being *without distinction*.

It is God who justifies. We don't need to justify ourselves, and indeed we cannot, so we can just stop trying. It is God who justifies; it is Christ Jesus who died, who was raised, who sits at the right hand of God, where he intercedes for us. Can we get our minds around this picture? Our Lord himself, who died for us, is the one who pleads our case against the accusing Powers.

"Who shall bring any charge against God's elect?" Who are

God's elect? It might seem obvious. But it is not so obvious. Who determines the worth and the destiny of each person? Each of us can probably think of someone by whom we would not want to be judged. Only one Judge counts. "Who is to condemn? It is Christ Jesus who ... intercedes for us." Only one Spirit counts. Only one Spirit can do the work of righteousness in us: the Holy Spirit, the third person of the blessed Trinity, who is at work in us who wait upon the Lord.

And what of the cosmos? What of the creation? How will it be freed from its bondage to futility and decay? Here is the great promise: Only one Victor will remain on the field when Sin and Death are overcome forever. He is the Lord of all, the one through whom God made all things, the one whose "word of power" preserves the universe against self-destruction (John 1:3; Heb. 1:2). "If God be for us, who shall be against us?" Can these things be against us: tribulation, distress, persecution, famine, nakedness, peril, sword? Can we be conquered by these things? Paul gives the signal of triumph: "No! In all these things we are *more than conquerors* through him who loved us." No, this is not about individual deaths. This is about a whole world of Death that has been undone in Christ.

Our Lord did not just offer himself as a sacrifice. He fought and won a battle against everything that would destroy us. That is why Paul is able to say that he is certain that neither death, nor life, nor angels, nor principalities, nor things present, nor things to come, nor powers, nor war, nor pandemics, nor terrorism, nor global warming, nor anything else in all creation, will be able to separate us from the love of God in Jesus Christ our Lord.

Nothing in all creation can defeat the redemptive purpose of God for all his creatures. None of us is beyond the reach of the one who has conquered. Each Christian plays a part in bearing witness to Christ's triumph. Make no mistake, all of us are in a war against the principalities and powers, but those who take arms against them fight on the winning side.

This is not about one person here and one person there dying and going to heaven. This is about the conquest of all that is out of joint in the world, and about the Spirit working through each of us to give out our own small signals that the future belongs to God. This gospel of Jesus Christ is about the remaking of the entire creation according to the purpose of the one who called it into being in the beginning and will bring it to fulfillment in the End.

PRAYER

O God, the protector of all that trust in thee, without whom nothing is strong, nothing is holy: Increase and multiply upon us thy mercy; that, thou being our ruler and guide, we may so pass through things temporal, that we finally lose not the things eternal; through Jesus Christ our Lord, who liveth and reigneth with thee and the Holy Spirit, one God, for ever and ever. Amen.

Hebrews 12

Our God is a consuming fire.

—HEBREWS 12:29

In the reading today from the Epistle to the Hebrews, there are two word pictures. One is from the old covenant and one from the new. The first scene shows the children of Israel gathered at the foot of Mount Sinai. The mountaintop is blazing with volcanic fire, so that even the redoubtable Moses is fearful of the manifestation of the power, majesty, wrath, and judgment of God. The celebrated American writer Annie Dillard loved passages like this. She wrote one like it herself: "Why do we people in churches seem like cheerful ... tourists on a package tour of the Absolute? ... On the whole I do not find Christians, outside of the catacombs, sufficiently sensible [aware] of conditions. Does anyone have the foggiest idea what sort of power we so blithely invoke? It is madness to wear ladies' straw hats and velvet hats to church; we should all be wearing crash helmets."[42]

The second word picture painted by the biblical writer shows us a different mountain, Mount Zion, the coming kingdom of God. He envisions the celestial city where "the angels and archangels and all the company of heaven" are gathered around the throne of the Son of God: "You have come to Mount Zion ... the city of the living God, the heavenly Jerusalem, [with] innumerable angels in festal gathering, and to the assembly of the first-born who are enrolled in heaven, and to a judge who is God of all, and to the spirits of the righteous made perfect, and to Jesus, the mediator of a new covenant" (Heb. 12:22–24).

At first glance, these two pictures might seem to be contrasting the God of the Old Testament with the God of the New Testament. But notice how the author of Hebrews links the two visions, first, by referring to God as "the judge who is God of all," and then by the last sentence of the passage: "Our God is a consuming fire." It's the same God. The God of Abraham, Isaac, and Jacob (the God of the Old Testament) and the God and Father of our Lord Jesus Christ (the God of the New Testament) are not two gods, but one God. There are not two gods, one wrathful and one loving, but one God who is Judge of all. "Therefore," says Hebrews, "let us offer to God acceptable worship, with reverence and awe" (12:28). The writer wants his readers to know "what sort of power they so blithely invoke." That's really the thrust of the passage; we are to understand that the God who has promised to gather his people into a great "cloud of witnesses" through the blood of Jesus is the same God whose judgment upon sin and death is felt as a consuming fire.

You see, the world was not created to be the way it is. We are not supposed to be reading and hearing bad news every day. The world is not supposed to be filled with earthquake, fire, and flood, with plague, pestilence, and famine (to use the language of the older Book of Common Prayer). Oil spills were not part of our Creator's plan for our planet. Cancer was not part of his plan for humanity. Murderous drug cartels were not part of his plan, and the rapacious American appetite for cocaine that keeps the cartels in business was not part of his plan. Is it not good news that God will judge all of this?

But the Hebrews passage gives us a more complete picture of the wrongs that need to be made right. On Mount Zion, we see Jesus, now reigning from heaven, "the mediator of a new covenant, [with his] sprinkled blood that speaks a better word than the blood of Abel" (12:24). Let's look at that. What's Abel got to do with this? This reference to Abel reminds us of what happened immediately after the fall of Adam and Eve, the first disobedience. Just in case we might think that being kicked out of the garden of Eden wasn't necessarily the worst thing that could happen, we are told that Cain killed his own brother, Abel, for no reason except jealousy. Ever since that cosmic disaster, the blood of Abel has cried out for justice.

But where is that justice to come from? Where is the power that *not only* can defeat cancer, heal the planet, and overcome our murderous instincts *but also* is able to make everything right again and restore what was lost?

The first two verses of Psalm 71 say this:

> In thee, O Lord, do I take refuge;
>   let me never be put to shame!
> In thy righteousness deliver me and rescue me;
>   incline thy ear to me, and save me! (Ps. 71:1–2)

Throughout the Psalms it is continually repeated: God is the one who saves, the one who is powerful to deliver. God alone can make right what is wrong. God alone can overcome death and the demons.

Look again at Hebrews: "You have come to Mount Zion and to the city of the living God, the heavenly Jerusalem...and to a judge who is God of all, and to the souls of the righteous made perfect, and to Jesus, the mediator of a new covenant, and to the sprinkled blood that speaks more graciously than the blood of Abel." The blood of Abel has been crying out for justice and righteousness from the first day until now, but that cry has been answered. It has been answered by the blood of Christ.

Jesus is the one who took our shame upon himself on the cross, on our behalf and in our place. He is the pioneer who has run the race ahead of us, who perfects our faith, and—from his

seat at the right hand of God—who will come in glory to be
the Judge of this whole world of sin and death. It is his blood
that speaks more graciously than the blood of Abel or even the
blood of the martyrs—more graciously because God alone is
able, through Christ, to make right everything that has been
wrong.

And so, our great and unconquerable hope is this: sin and
the demons will be judged and consumed by the Lord himself.
That will happen in his time, which is not ours to know. But in
the meantime, the powers of death will be judged a little bit at
a time as God works through the deeds of love and mercy done
by his people, by all who stand alongside others in suffering
and who work for justice and righteousness.

PRAYER

O Lord, we beseech thee, let thy continual pity cleanse and
defend thy Church; and, because it cannot continue in safety
without thy succor, preserve it evermore by thy help and goodness; through Jesus Christ our Lord, who liveth and reigneth
with thee and the Holy Spirit, one God, for ever and ever.
Amen.

Romans 3:9; 7:15–21

All human beings are under the power of sin.

—ROMANS 3:9

I n any polarized situation, the overriding human tendency is to draw a line with oneself and one's allies on the good side and the opposing party on the wicked side, with very little attempt made by either side to understand the other. As these positions harden, it becomes almost impossible to achieve the insight necessary for a breakthrough. For some years now I have kept a file that I call "The Line Runs Through." This title is from Václav Havel, former president of the Czech Republic and one of those who resisted the Communists and was put in prison for his activities. When he came to power after the "Velvet Revolution," Havel was conspicuously forgiving toward his former enemies and other collaborators. Some blamed him for this, but he maintained his position. In the central European regimes of the seventies and eighties, Havel said, "The line [between good and evil] did not run clearly between 'them' and 'us,' but through each person."[43]

The line between good and evil runs through each person. Listen to Saint Paul: "I do not understand my own actions. For I do not do what I want, but I do the very thing I hate.... I can will what is right, but I cannot do it. For I do not do the good I want, but the evil I do not want is what I do. Now if I do what I do not want, it is no longer I that do it, but sin which dwells within me. So I find it to be a law that when I want to do right, evil lies close at hand" (Rom. 7:15–21). Is there anyone who does not recognize this?

The human being is in the grip of impulses that are more powerful than our wish to do good. Our Lord wants us to know of the power of these forces. In the words of Jesus in the Gospels, in the writings of Saint Paul, we are told over and over in various ways that the powers we face are untiring, malevolent, and extremely clever. These powers seek nothing less than our destruction. But we are not defenseless. The apostle counsels us:

> Put on the whole armor of God, that you may be able to stand against the wiles of the devil. For we are not contending against flesh and blood, but against the principalities, against the powers, against the world rulers of this present darkness, against the spiritual hosts of wickedness in the heavenly places. (Eph. 6:11–12)

The forces that we face are overwhelming, and the suffering that they cause is incalculable. The Christian should not be deceived about this. Jesus wants us to know ahead of time that the Christian life is going to be a long struggle against evil, sin, and death—most of all, the evil, sin, and death that threaten our own being.

It is important that we use the word "we" when we say the Confession in the worship service. Human solidarity in bondage to the power of sin is one of the most important of all concepts for Christians to grasp. At the same time, though, saying the words of the Confession communally in church does not always cause us to appropriate its truth deep in our being. All of us need to say also (in the words of Thomas Cranmer's General Confession), "I have erred and strayed from God's ways like a lost sheep. I have followed too much the devices and desires of *my own* heart." This is not so easy for us. All of us, to one degree or another, participate in that psychological phenomenon famously called *denial*. Denial, or avoidance, is a way of keeping consciousness of sin at bay. We think we can make sin go away by pretending it is not there; we are like the little girl who says, "I've got my eyes closed so nobody can see me."

The line between good and evil runs through each person. The truly tragic person is the one who causes harm and never repents of it, never admits it even internally. That person is blocked from receiving the promise of the gospel that God's grace is retroactive. If it weren't, the promise it holds out to us would be empty. God's power is able to make right all that has happened in the past. Paul seldom uses the word "forgiveness." His stronger word is "justification." Justification means that we sinners will not only be *forgiven*, we will be *justified*, which means that we will be set right by the power of God, and all who have suffered as a result of our faults will have perfect restitution.

How can this be?

The sacrifice of Jesus our Lord is this: he has gone into the day of judgment utterly alone, separated from the Father, taking the sentence of condemnation upon himself, bearing it away from us. This is the gospel. This is the good news of the Christian faith. Neutrality is no longer possible. Satan is slashing and burning, but he is in retreat. His time will come. There is no longer any room for self-deception, excuses, denial, or evasion, for, as C. S. Lewis puts it, "Fallen man is not simply an imperfect creature who needs improvement; he is a rebel who must lay down his arms."[44] It is the Lord Jesus Christ who disarms us.

But listen: we are not *disarmed* in order to be *disempowered*. There is "power in the blood of the Lamb." It is the power of the Word of God that spoke, *and it was so*. It is the power that overcame Satan in the wilderness. It is the power that lifted the paralyzed man to his feet. It is the power that spoke through the voice of the Son of God when he said, "Peace! Be still!" and the wind and waves obeyed their Creator. It is the power that sustains every Christian in the struggles of this life.

This power is able to do things that we can only dream about. For this is the might of the God in whom Abraham believed, the God whose power "raises the dead and calls into existence the things that do not exist" (Rom. 4:17). The God who reckoned Abraham righteous is the God who justifies sinners. For the righteousness reckoned to Abraham was *not for his sake alone but for ours also.* The promise of God to sinners today is that "it will be reckoned to us who believe in him that raised from the dead Jesus our Lord" (Rom. 4:24).

PRAYER

Grant to us, Lord, we beseech thee, the spirit to think and do always such things as are right, that we, who cannot exist without thee, may by thee be enabled to live according to thy will; through Jesus Christ our Lord, who liveth and reigneth with thee and the Holy Spirit, one God, for ever and ever. *Amen.*

Romans 5

If, because of one man's trespass, death reigned through that one man, much more will those who receive the abundance of grace and the free gift of righteousness reign in life through the one man Jesus Christ.

—ROMANS 5:17

In chapter 5 of the Epistle to the Romans, Saint Paul, with all the considerable passion of which he was capable, writes of the danger that the whole world is in and the mortal peril that Christian believers have narrowly escaped. He is attempting to send a message to the church—in order to see what the human race has gained in Christ, we must understand the terrible destiny that would have been ours.

Paul is very clear about the ubiquitous force of Sin. He personifies Sin in his writings, as though it were a reigning monarch (as indeed it is): "Sin won dominion" over all men, he says.[45] He depicts Sin with its favorite and characteristic weapon, Death, forcefully advancing through the world like an annihilating army (and it is like that): "Sin came into the world ... and death through sin, and so death spread to all men because all men sinned" (5:12), and the consequence is that "Sin gained domination through death." This means that we actually live in a domain of sin, a realm of death from which there is no escape whatsoever.

Paul assumes that all his readers know the story in Genesis: Adam was created by God and placed in the garden of Eden with a choice—Adam could choose to live in perfect harmony with God, with Eve, and with himself, free from sin. Adam chose instead to disobey God, and from that time on, there has been no choice. No one has been able to choose to live outside the iron rule of Sin and Death. God has "handed us over," as Paul writes in Romans 1. "Sin entered the world through one man [Adam], and death through sin, and so death spread to all men because all men sinned." The contagion of Adam's disobedience has caused the disobedience of the entire race of human beings.

Adam and Jesus Christ. Each man determines a world: Adam's world is the world of sin and death; Christ's world is the world of new life and true freedom given by God. Adam's world originates in rebellion against God the Creator; the new world in Jesus Christ originates in the grace of the heavenly Father, and it is made effective through the obedience of Jesus, which swallows up our disobedience in victory.

Paul is trying to tell us that our life in Christ has been snatched out of the jaws of death. He is grabbing us, so to speak, and urgently telling us the story of our deliverance. And he knows that unless and until we make this story our own, it will never be for us anything more than a story told at second hand by someone whose experience we have not shared.

It is critically important to recognize that the effectiveness of Paul's argument is not dependent upon his ability to convince people of the bad situation they are in. It is God's grace that illuminates the terror of our previous case. We recognize the enormity of the threat that hung over us only when we recognize that we are safe. Then we collapse in gratitude. Paul wishes above all to enable us to be thus overcome by thanksgiving and joy. Then we want to tell the story to everyone and draw them into it too.

As you can see in the text, Paul is building up an argument from the lesser to the greater. "How much more," he says, does Christ's action of grace save us. "How much more" powerful and victorious Christ is than Adam was. "That one man," Adam, drew the whole human race into rebellion along with him; "how much more" does "that one man," Jesus Christ, give "the abundance of grace and the free gift of righteousness." I can't prove this to you, any more than Paul could. We know these things only by faith in Christ, "that one man."

Narrow escape is an impossible experience to convey to those who are not aware that they, too, have been snatched back from the brink of the abyss. The life of Adam is precarious in the extreme. We are threatened at every turn by disease, crime, loss, accident, intrusion, insanity, terror; what is even worse, we are threatened by condemnation—exposure of what we really are, rejection by those whose love we most need, ultimate abandonment by God himself. Humanly speaking, this is our inheritance.

Paul says, this is what we have narrowly escaped! Jesus Christ, the Son of the God who is our Judge, has come to our rescue. He has quite literally appeared on the human scene with divine power to save. It is an unparalleled drama of desperate peril and miraculous deliverance—and it is not only my story, but your story.

Paul wants more than anything else in the world for us to recognize our Savior, "the one man Jesus Christ," the one in whom we are liberated once and for all, set on our way, incorporated into the resurrection life of God, transferred from the dominion of death into the dominion of the Messiah and his victory over every form of evil.

There is only one Savior who was not born into the dominion of Adam. Only one. That one man, Jesus Christ, is alone able to redeem us for a life free from the dominion of Sin and Death. In him alone, in that one man alone, is joy, peace, deliverance, acquittal, and a safe homecoming. In him only. In him alone. *That one man.*

That one name.

Jesus Christ.

PRAYER

Almighty God, who hast given thy only Son to be unto us both a sacrifice for sin and also an example of godly life: Give us grace that we may always most thankfully receive that his inestimable benefit, and also daily endeavor ourselves to follow the blessed steps of his most holy life; through the same Jesus Christ thy Son our Lord, who liveth and reigneth with thee and the Holy Spirit, one God, now and for ever. *Amen.*

FIFTEENTH SUNDAY AFTER PENTECOST

Ephesians 4:1–16

> There is one body and one Spirit ... one Lord, one faith, one baptism,
> one God and Father of us all.
>
> —EPHESIANS 4:4–6

You only need to turn on the news for a few minutes to see more evidence for the truth of the biblical teaching that the world needs to be saved. One way to interpret hard news is to conclude that there is no God and that human existence is a cruel joke. Some of the greatest writers and thinkers have come to this conclusion. I myself find it very difficult to defend faith in God in the face of senseless violence and suffering. As for finding answers, it is not only difficult, it is impossible. The Bible gives no answer to the problem of evil. It simply tells us that the whole world is in "bondage to decay" (Rom. 8:21) and that we are all "by nature children of wrath" (Eph. 2:3) and that the human race is deserving of condemnation.

The message of the Bible is that there is no rescue from within this sphere. Rescue must come from beyond. And that is exactly what has happened. "We all once lived in the passions of our flesh, following the desires of body and mind, and so we were by nature children of wrath, like the rest of mankind. But God, who is rich in mercy, out of the great love with which he loved us, even when we were dead through our trespasses, made us alive together with Christ—by grace you have been saved!" (Eph. 2:3–5). So now we proceed from

205

the great gospel message *Saved!* to the question, *Saved for what?*

The primary answer to the question "Saved for what?" is found repeated many times in the first chapter of Ephesians. We are saved *for the praise of his glory* (1:14). God's glory is not so much God's magnificence as it is his mercy. "In him we have redemption through his blood, the forgiveness of our trespasses, according to the riches of his grace which he lavished upon us" (1:7-8). Even more glorious, we will not just be forgiven, we will be transformed; we will be perfected. Paul says, "We [will] be holy and blameless before [God]" (1:4).

The saving grace of God is the beginning of a new story for us, the story of our passing from the world in which we are ruled by "the devices and desires of our own hearts" into the world of God's purposes. It is the story of our passing from the world where "we have left undone those things which we ought to have done, and we have done those things which we ought not to have done," into the new and hitherto unknown world where we are being made *holy and blameless* before God. That, we are told in the first chapter of Ephesians, is God's great plan.

But now comes another shocker. It is God's plan to accomplish the rescue of the world *through you and me!* Paul tells us in Ephesians that it is God's eternal purpose to make his new world come into being *through the church* (3:10-11). What a crazy idea! How can we take it seriously? I assure you this is one of the questions that troubles me most, in view of the church's dismal performance in many instances. Yet the apostolic message is clear.

In the fourth chapter of Ephesians, Paul says, "I ... beg you to lead a life worthy of the calling to which you have been called, with all lowliness and humility, with patience, forbearing one another in love, eager to maintain the unity of the Spirit in the bond of peace. There is one body and one Spirit ... one Lord, one faith, one baptism, one God and Father of us all" (4:1-6).

Here the apostle is thinking of the way that all Christian congregations are continually threatening to pull apart into factions. This must not be, he says, for there is only "one Lord, one faith, one baptism." Paul is not thinking here of the different denominations that we have today. He has in mind the cliques and parties that develop within all congregations. Wherever such divisions persist, the church is failing its commission. On the other hand, whenever there are renewed fellowship, deepening respect, developing affection, there are the signs that God's plan is working the way it is supposed to.

At the conclusion of our reading for today, Paul says, "Speaking the truth in love, we are to grow up in every way into him who is the head, into Christ, from whom the whole body, joined and knit together by every joint with which it is supplied, when each part is working properly, makes bodily growth and upbuilds itself in love" (4:15–16). Notice the phrase "when each part is working properly." Paul is not into denial. He recognizes that, more often than not, the church will not be "working properly." But he knows that when it does work properly, everyone will recognize it and will be exhilarated by it.

The Christian community, when it is *working properly*, offers men and women a way of being related to one another that cuts across all the things that divide us. It is the church and only the church, when it is working properly, that is "joined and knit together in every joint, that makes bodily growth and upbuilds itself in love" across every barrier of race, age, class, and experience. There is nothing else in human life that levels distinctions and creates new relationships like the knowledge that one has been saved by grace.

"By grace you have been saved." Saved for what? Here's what. Saved to be a beachhead for God's great reclamation project to save the world from sin and death. Saved to be a dwelling place of God's unconditional love for sinners of every description. Saved to be messengers of the gospel of Christ not only with our lips but also in our lives. Saved to beat our "swords into plowshares, and our spears into pruning hooks" (Isa. 2:4) for a new kind of warfare whose colors will never be put into a museum or stored in an attic or relegated to a closet, but will grow brighter as they are united with the victorious majesty of our Lord Jesus Christ forever and ever. As one hymn puts it, "For not with swords' loud clashing, nor roll of stirring drums, but deeds of love and mercy, the heavenly kingdom comes."[46]

Saved for what? Saved to live in this life in such a way that, in the life to come, our severed friendships will be restored to an intimacy and ease that we can only now begin to imagine; we shall dance and sing in harmony forever to the praise of God's glorious grace.

PRAYER

Grant, we beseech thee, merciful God, that thy Church, being gathered together in unity by thy Holy Spirit, may manifest thy power among all peoples, to the glory of thy Name; through Jesus Christ our Lord, who liveth and reigneth with thee and the Holy Spirit, one God, world without end. *Amen.*

Mark 9:14-29

Jesus said to him, "If you can! All things are possible to him who believes." Immediately the father of the child cried out and said, "I believe; help my unbelief!"

—MARK 9:23-24

How much do you have to believe to be a bona fide Christian? What is a believer? What is an unbeliever? Which are you? Don't jump to conclusions too quickly; just because a person is sitting in a church pew doesn't necessarily mean the person is of great faith. A lot of people are hanging on by the thinnest of threads.

There used to be more certainty about the content of Christian faith than there is today. Children used to learn their catechisms and memorize Scripture. These days, it seems as though believers can believe just about anything, making it up as they go along. Vaguely general ideas of religion and "spirituality" threaten to replace orthodoxy. I heard a sermon once in which the preacher exhorted us for fifteen minutes to have faith without ever saying a single word about what we were supposed to have faith in. Surely, however, we cannot avoid the issue indefinitely. And so the question becomes, faith in what? Belief in what? And does it matter?

In Mark's Gospel, chapter 9, Jesus has just come down off the Mount of Transfiguration where Peter, James, and John "beheld his glory, glory as of the only Son from the Father"

(John 1:14). Our Lord wastes no time soaking up these divine rays, however. Before you know it, they are all coming down off the mountain and Jesus is plunged into the midst of yet another controversy. He finds his disciples in the midst of a large crowd, contending with the established teachers of religion.

Jesus asks the disputants, "What are you discussing?" (Mark 9:16). One of the men present promptly speaks up and takes responsibility for setting off the conflict. "Teacher," he says. "I brought my son to you, for he has a dumb spirit; and wherever it seizes him, it dashes him down; and he foams and grinds his teeth and becomes rigid; and I asked your disciples to cast it out, and they were not able" (vv. 17–18).

He has brought his son to Jesus's disciples hoping for help, but their failure has caused him to lose most of that hope. His words to Jesus clearly show that he isn't expecting much at this stage. He says, "[The evil spirit] has often cast him into the fire and into the water, *to destroy him*; but *if you can do anything*, have pity on us and help us" (v. 22). From these words, we see that we are looking at a human life about to be obliterated by an evil power, and we are aware that the father is very doubtful of Jesus's ability to do anything about it. The outcome hangs here, on this point. Heaven and earth hold their breath. The demon has already deployed his weapons; the boy is thrashing about in a terrifying fashion.

Jesus can vanquish the evil power with a mere word. But he delays. The disciples have failed, the teachers of the law look on scornfully, the crowd hangs back in bemusement, no longer certain what to expect as the Master draws out the dialogue with the father by repeating his own doubtful words back to him: "'If you can do anything!' All things are possible to him who believes." And immediately the father of the boy cries out and says, "I believe; help my unbelief!" (vv. 23–24).

In a split second the father has been seized by hope. He has been seized by life. He has been seized by the power of God. And the father's corresponding action is to grasp with all his might at the giver of hope and life and healing power. He puts himself into Jesus's hands totally. In words that have been called the greatest cry of faith in the entire Bible, he places himself under the mercy and mastery of the Lord. "I believe; help my unbelief!" The instant is electric.

Jesus utters his command with the most emphatic possible stress on his own unique authority: "Thou dumb and deaf spirit, I charge thee, come out of him, and enter into him no more"—whereupon the demon, uttering a terrible cry of rage and defeat, convulses the boy terribly and flees from him.

"All things are possible to him who believes." Believes what? Believes that all things are possible? Believes in faith healing? Believes in belief? No. All commentators agree: the faith that is evoked by Jesus's dialogue with the father is not assent to any theological proposition. It is not agreement with any religious principle. It is not acquiescence in any spiritual program. It is radical trust in the person of Jesus, the one "who calls into existence the things that do not exist" (Rom. 4:17), the one who creates faith where there is no faith.

Through the retelling of this story, Jesus Christ the Lord has arranged a meeting between himself and you. He is not waiting for you to figure it all out. He is not lying back observing to see if you have enough faith. He is not withholding his approval pending your successful application. He has come forward to meet you, in word and sacrament. The only person with perfect faith is Jesus Christ. When he says, "All things are possible to him who believes," there is a sense in which he speaks first of himself. It is by his faith, his faithfulness, that we receive our own faith. There is no foundation more certain than that.

Are you a believer or an unbeliever? No matter how troubling your doubts may be, no matter how inadequate you may feel compared to others, no matter how often you may feel that you are just going through the motions, you would not be here reading if you did not have some germ of faith, however small.

That is the Holy Spirit of Christ already at work in you. It is enough. Trust the Lord of faith to make it grow.

PRAYER

Lord of all power and might, who art the author and giver of all good things: Graft in our hearts the love of thy Name; increase in us true religion; nourish us with all goodness; and bring forth in us the fruit of good works; through Jesus Christ our Lord, who liveth and reigneth with thee and the Holy Spirit, one God, for ever and ever. *Amen.*

Romans 1:16; 8:1–4

For I am not ashamed of the gospel.

—ROMANS 1:16

Paul was a man of towering intellectual stature and considerable privilege. He was not only a Pharisee of the highest class, he was also a Roman citizen—and that was no mean thing in those days. Paul could have remained rich, republican, and religious all his life and died peacefully in bed. But something happened to him. On the road to Damascus, where he was headed with the intention of persecuting and even killing members of the new Christian faith, he was knocked from his horse with the force of a blow by the living Jesus Christ, and his entire world outlook was revolutionized.

All during his missionary years Paul knew exactly what the elites thought of him and the new faith. Jews called it scandalous (Greek *skandalon*, stumbling block) and gentiles called it foolishness (1 Cor. 1:23). The "wise men," the great orators and philosophers, the religion professors all ridiculed the gospel of Christ crucified, "but God has chosen what is foolish in the world to shame the wise" (1 Cor. 1:27). So when Paul preaches the gospel, you see, he connects the two words "foolishness" and "gospel." He writes in his introduction to Romans, "I am under obligation both to Greeks and to barbarians, both to the wise and to the *foolish*: so I am eager to preach the *gospel* to you also who are in Rome. For I am not ashamed of the gospel."

Now to all those who are affluent churchgoers, the unvar-
nished gospel of Christ crucified still presents itself under the
heading of *foolishness.* The gospel that Paul preached, the gospel
that set the Mediterranean world afire, the gospel preached
to the gentiles by this unworthy but God-sent apostle—this
gospel, when preached in its undiluted form, has never fit into
any of the world's molds. It does not bring "happiness" as the
world understands happiness. It does not bring riches or status
or guarantees of worldly security. It brings accusations: "Why
are you hanging around with those born-again people?" "You
brought my dinner party to a dead halt with your embarrass-
ing testimony." To which Paul replies, for all days and all ages,
"I am not ashamed of the gospel. It is the power of God for
salvation."

Now let's jump to the reading from chapter 8 of Romans.
Paul's language is often dense and difficult to understand, but
once you catch on to it, it blasts you with joyful good news. In
this passage Paul is contrasting two kinds of law. The *first* kind
is the law that condemns people and imprisons them without
hope—he calls that the law of the flesh, or the law of sin and
death.

The *second* kind of law is the law of the Spirit that creates
new life. Our Lord Jesus Christ, Paul says, was born into the
realm of the flesh, that is, the realm of the first kind of law—the
law that judges, condemns, and executes. That's why he was
crucified. He took upon himself the condemnation of the law
that hands human beings over to trial and judgment and execution. He suffered and died under this law, the law that says
it's all right to torture people to death if it's in a good cause.

But there is another kind of law, the law that connects the
good commandments of God the Father with the new life of
God the Holy Spirit. Paul declares that when our Lord died
under the law of sin, he was fulfilling in his own body—his
own flesh—the just requirement of God's law. I know this is
hard to understand at first, but once you get it you will never

forget it. In the cross of Christ, *retributive justice*—the law that condemns—is put to death and is replaced by *restorative justice*—the law that gives life. You and I disobey the Ten Commandments every day of the week, but in him, because he was perfectly righteous, the just requirement of the law is fulfilled *for us* and, Paul writes, *in us*—so that we are enabled, by his grace, to move into and live the new life of the Spirit.

The action of the Holy Spirit in all this is to make Christ's saving death present and powerful in the lives of sinners. By the agency of the Spirit, there is a new creation. The role of the Spirit is elaborated in the Gospel of John. The Spirit is called the Paraclete, a Greek word meaning *advocate*, or lawyer for the defense. At God's bar of judgment, the Holy Spirit is your defense counsel.

C. S. Lewis gave a wonderful title to a chapter in one of his books: "Nice People, or New Men?"[47] His point was that the gospel does not confer blessings upon nice people. The gospel radically challenges "nice" people to become *new* people, new creations, people who by the power of the Spirit are being changed into the likeness of Christ.

Think now of yourself. Somebody somewhere does not want you to be a new person in Jesus Christ, let alone "born again." It would embarrass that person. Or maybe the person would even like to see you in trouble. The useful German word *Schadenfreude* identifies this universal human trait—taking pleasure in the troubles of others. Somewhere out there, someone is feeling that way about you. Maybe it's a person you blackballed, or a person you fired, or a person you wronged. Maybe that person is your rival in business, or your first wife, or even one of your children. Somewhere there is someone who does not want you to be a new person.

But life in the Holy Spirit means not being ashamed of the gospel of the new birth. It means dying to the standards of this world. It means not caring if your fellow sinners are embarrassed by you, or even if your friends and family are embarrassed by you, because you have an Advocate with the Father. "The law of the Spirit of life in Christ Jesus has set me free from the law of sin and death" (8:2). The just requirement of the law has been fulfilled in us by the death of Jesus Christ. That, truly, is restorative justice. We no longer live "according to the flesh but according to the Spirit" (8:4). There is a whole new world open to us, a world in which God does not weigh our merits but pardons our offenses[48]—and then rebuilds our lives according to "the law of the Spirit of life in Christ Jesus."

> For I am not ashamed of the gospel.... There is therefore now no condemnation for those who are in Christ Jesus.

PRAYER

O God, forasmuch as without thee we are not able to please thee, mercifully grant that thy Holy Spirit may in all things direct and rule our hearts; through Jesus Christ our Lord, who with thee and the same Spirit liveth and reigneth, one God, now and for ever. *Amen.*

Matthew 13:24–30, 36–43; Romans 8:12–25

> *"'Let both grow together until the harvest; and at harvest time I will tell the reapers, Gather the weeds first and bind them in bundles to be burned, but gather the wheat into my barn.'"*

—MATTHEW 13:30

When Jesus told the parable of the wheat and the tares, he began, "The kingdom of God is like …" So many of Jesus's stories begin that way. He doesn't describe the kingdom of God directly. He gives homely illustrations from real life.

Earlier generations of American Christians were very familiar with this image of the harvest as the final ingathering of God's children. They loved hymns like "Bringing in the Sheaves," and at Thanksgiving sang, "Come, ye thankful people, come, raise the song of harvest home." Everyone understood that didn't just mean food in the pantry; it meant *we ourselves* were to be the fruitful ears of corn and wheat. This is what Jesus has in mind with his image.

There is an extra edge in the parable, though, that isn't so folksy. Our Lord is thinking of the decidedly nonpastoral figure of John the Baptist. Earlier in the Gospel of Matthew, John declares, "He who is coming after me is mightier than I, whose sandals I am not worthy to carry. … His winnowing fork is in his hand, and he will clear his threshing floor and gather his wheat into the granary, but the chaff he will burn with unquenchable fire" (3:11-12). Matthew places this early in his

gospel to indicate that Jesus himself is the Lord of the final harvest, the one who will be the Judge of good and evil in the last
day. When you realize that some of Jesus's original audience
would have actually heard John's preaching, you get a better
idea of the drama in Jesus's repeated claim that "the kingdom
of God is at hand," meaning that he himself is bringing it.[49]

By the time Matthew wrote all this down, some time had
gone by. The early Christians were trying to figure out how to
coexist with a world that was hostile to the gospel of the Son of
God. This led to a lot of questions. If Jesus was truly the Son of
God, why had not the kingdom arrived in its plenitude? What
sort of attitude were Christians supposed to have toward evil
in their midst? Why did God allow Satan to rampage around
sowing weeds?

This leads us from the parable to Paul. One of the trickiest
problems in all biblical interpretation is the relation between
the teaching of Jesus and that of Paul. Paul is often thought of
as the spoiler who took the simple lessons of Jesus and made
them intellectual, abstract, harsh, and—God forbid—theological. It comes as a shock to many to realize that there is far
more teaching about judgment, condemnation, hellfire, and
good people versus bad people in the words of Jesus than in
the letters of Paul.

Indeed, if it were not for Paul, we might not have known
how to place the emphasis in many of Jesus's stories. In today's
parable, for example, the point sure seems to be that there are
good people and bad people, and the bad ones are going to be
firewood in the end. It is Paul, obliquely if not directly, who
keeps reminding us that Jesus habitually kept company with
tax collectors and prostitutes, and that he "came not to call the
righteous, but sinners" (Matt. 9:13)—because it is Paul who explains, in chapters 2 and 3 of Romans, that "there is none righteous, no, not one ... all human beings, both Jews and Gentiles,
are under the power of sin" (Rom. 3:9–10).

In Shakespeare's play All's Well That Ends Well, two young

French lords are speaking together about the ambiguities of the other characters' actions. One says to the other, "The web of our life is of a mingled yarn, good and ill together."[50] Thus, in the parable of Jesus, the landowner says, "Let both weeds and wheat grow together until the harvest."

Criminals, slave owners, tax collectors, prostitutes, vestry members, deacons, elders, clergy, Pharisees, tobacco executives, faculty, students, adulterers, idolaters—here we all are growing along together by the grace of God. Who is to say who is good and who is bad? It is the Lord who will make the distinction. And make it he will. In the end, that is the principal thrust of the parable. There will be a separation, just as John the Baptist said, and the Son of God will make it. The enemy will be destroyed. Sin will be overcome. Evil will be rooted out for all time. I look forward to the day when the evil in my own soul will be rooted out.

John the Baptist made one mistake. He thought the Messiah was going to swing the scythe of judgment as soon as he appeared. We get the feeling that John was sort of looking forward to seeing the bad people polished off. He had expected the Coming One to execute judgment on evildoers as his first act. It had not yet been revealed to John that the judgment would be executed in a way that no one expected. The last thing he could have imagined was that Jesus Christ would undergo the judgment himself.

It is Paul the apostle who lays out before us the paradox of God's mercy revealed in his judgment, the promise of deliverance even in the midst of suffering, the hope of redemption beyond condemnation. He summons up a cosmic picture in which all humanity, believers and unbelievers alike, and the whole created order participate together both in the suffering and in the hope, as we wait for the final harvest: "The whole creation has been groaning in travail together until now; and not only the creation, but we ourselves, who have the first fruits of the Spirit, groan inwardly as we wait for adoption as sons, the redemption of our bodies. For in this hope we were saved" (Rom. 8:22–24). When Jesus the Judge comes again, that will be the Great Day when the "heaven door" will swing open, yes, not just for the pious and the polished but for "lives of mingled yarn" everywhere, yes, even for prisoners and sinners like you and me.

PRAYER

O God, who declarest thy almighty power chiefly in showing mercy and pity: Mercifully grant unto us such a measure of thy grace, that we, running to obtain thy promises, may be made partakers of thy heavenly treasure; through Jesus Christ our Lord, who liveth and reigneth with thee and the Holy Spirit, one God, for ever and ever. *Amen.*

2 Kings 5:1–19

> [Naaman] *was a mighty man of valor, but he was a leper.*
>
> —2 KINGS 5:1

N aaman the Syrian was a five-star general of the army. He was commander of all the armed forces of the king of Syria. The troops under him had achieved massive victories. We're told that "Naaman was a mighty man of valor." All Damascus stood in awe of him. He could walk right into the king's throne room without an appointment. He had his choice of limousines and secretaries and uniforms with gold braid. There was just one problem. "Naaman was a mighty man of valor—but he was a leper" (2 Kings 5:1).

The CEO of the huge multinational corporation can get the best table at Four Seasons without even calling for a reservation—but his son was hospitalized last year for a suicide attempt. The famous professor is in great demand all over the world for lectures at fees in the five figures—but he's an alcoholic. The celebrated actress can cause every man's head to turn just by walking into the room—but she lives in dread of bright lights and mirrors set at unflattering angles. The beloved pastor brings joy and hope into dozens of lives daily—but his wife despises him. In every life there is a *but*. What is your *but*? What is my *but*? Naaman was a great man with his master and in high favor . . . he was a mighty man of valor, *but he was a leper.*

Now, you understand, ancient society knew no treatment for Naaman's horrifying disease. Even more important, the Bible presents leprosy as a metaphor for guilt, sin, and death. That's why there's a *but* in your life and a *but* in mine. "Naaman was in high favor . . . but he was a leper." No cure, no remedy, no treatment. *Leprosy* is a metaphor for all that is diseased and wrong in human life, for all that is hopeless, for all that is shameful, for all that we seek to keep hidden, even from ourselves, lest the miserable truth be known.

But then—a young woman, a foreigner, a slave, a nobody speaks a word of hope from another world. "Would that my lord were with the prophet who is in Samaria! He would cure him of his leprosy" (5:3).

You just read the story; you know what happens. Naaman makes his way eventually to Elisha with all his horses, chariots, men, money, and all the rest of it. Note that Naaman simply "halts at the door"; he waits haughtily for the prophet to come out to him. No doubt he believed the prophet would be very impressed and honored by his visit. Naaman regarded it as Elisha's duty to come out to him, Elisha being his social inferior.

But Elisha does not come out. Instead, he sends his servant to the door with a brief message for the general: "Go and wash in the Jordan seven times, and your flesh shall be restored, and you shall be clean" (5:10). And Naaman, we are told, "turned and went away in a rage"—and Elisha does not raise a finger to hold him back. Elisha, in fact—like Yahweh, whom he serves—remains invisible, permitting Naaman this liberty to turn away from deliverance. There is no sign from heaven, no thunderbolt, no voice from the sky saying, "Naaman! Go back! This is God speaking!"

Instead, once again, the story turns upon the voice of a nobody. Naaman's servants—not his lieutenants, not his advisers, but his *servants*!—sidle up to him hesitantly. And notice the simplicity and the theological inadequacy of their argument.

We do not expect God to work in this way; Naaman certainly did not. He had thought that Elisha would come out to him and make dramatic gestures and utter eloquent words and treat him in a way that befitted his station in life.

But somehow Naaman is enabled to see some sense in the hesitant speech of his servants. He goes down and dips himself seven times in the Jordan, according to the word of the man of God; and his flesh is restored like the flesh of a little child, and he is clean (5:14).

And behold! Naaman the Syrian gets back on his horse and gives the command to his entourage to follow, and he goes all the way back to the house of Elisha, and this time Naaman gets down off his horse, and this time Elisha comes right out to meet him, and Naaman makes his confession: "Now I know that there is no God in all the earth except in Israel" (5:15).

Now: think of Naaman for a moment from the standpoint of the Hebrew people, who remembered hearing this story and eventually wrote it down. Naaman was a Syrian—a man of another race, another culture, not one of the chosen people. Naaman was a pagan, an unbeliever, a man who couldn't have cared less for the God of Israel. He was more than that: he was the leader of the forces of Israel's enemies, of the opposing ideology, the hostile nation. And Naaman was certainly not one of the poor whom God loves, not one of the humble, not one of the lowly.

God is, as always, one step ahead of us with his grace. Just as we think we know who it is whom God loves (us), he reaches beyond us and brings an outsider like Naaman into his fold. We do not want to believe that God shows preferential treatment to the foreigners, the pagans, the enemy—let alone an enemy of the ruling class.

How does God show his love to humanity? It would seem that he does it without regard for either rich or poor. Even more drastically, he extends his mercy and works out his plan, more often than not, through the little slave girls and the stammering servants of this world, through the prophets who seek no glory for themselves but remain anonymously in the background.

There is someone somewhere in your life, bearing a word of hope for your leprosy, for your *but*. It may be someone you are very jealous of, or very threatened by, or very scornful of. And the message, when you hear it, will almost invariably offend you by its simplicity, its unexpectedness, its lack of appropriateness as the world understands such things. God shows his love not by overwhelming us with demonstrations of power and majesty, not by clubbing us to our knees, not by staging exhibitions of supernatural strength such as we humans might expect God to do, but rather by coming alongside us with water, and bread, and wine, and the invitation:

> Wash, and be clean;
> follow me, and be healed;
> take and eat this, and be fed with the bread from heaven;
> drink this, and you will never be thirsty again.

PRAYER

Almighty and everlasting God, who art always more ready to hear than we to pray, and art wont to give more than either we desire or deserve: Pour down upon us the abundance of thy mercy, forgiving us those things whereof our conscience is afraid, and giving us those good things which we are not worthy to ask, but through the merits and mediation of Jesus Christ thy Son our Lord; who liveth and reigneth with thee and the Holy Spirit, one God, for ever and ever. *Amen.*

Isaiah 45

Truly, thou art a God who hidest thyself.

—ISAIAH 45:15

The prophet Isaiah's words "Truly, thou art a God who hidest thyself" have had a lot of attention over the centuries. Throughout Christian history, the question has always been asked: "When terrible things happen, where is God?" It becomes more urgent and more agonizing when something happens to children. When the news of the massacre at the Newtown, Connecticut, elementary school came through, there wasn't, or shouldn't have been, a Christian believer in this country who didn't ask, "Where was God? Why does God permit these atrocities?"

This is the question that Christian faith must ask. It's a very shallow faith if it does not ask. Unfortunately, many people have been conditioned *not to ask* these kinds of questions— as though they were disrespectful, or intrusive, or dangerous. There's even an idea that asking such a question is like opening a door to not believing in God at all. But the people of the Bible *do* ask, directly and bluntly. The questions are asked over and over again in the Psalms. The wonderful little book of the prophet Habakkuk asks it this way: "Oh Lord, how long shall I cry for help and you will not hear? Why are you silent when the wicked man swallows up the one more righteous than he?" (Hab. 1:2, 13).

The silence of God, the absence of God, is a major theme of Scripture and the Christian life. Habakkuk's questions are part of every believer's struggle for faith. Anyone who has not asked this question hasn't been fully tested yet.

"Truly, thou art a God who hidest thyself." We need to understand here that God is not just hidden on general principles. If God is hidden, it is because he hides *himself*. He *means* to be hidden. It is God's nature to be out of the reach of our senses. There is a distance between God and ourselves that cannot be bridged from our side.

There are two different ways of asking, "Where is God? Why does God hide himself?" One way is scornful, hostile, and truly *God-less*, like the abuse and mockery hurled at Jesus on the cross: "He trusted in God to deliver him, so let God deliver him!" The people who yelled that insult thought they knew who God was and what God would and would not do (Matt. 27:43; also Ps. 22:8).

But the other way of asking comes from deep faith. It comes from having at least a partial knowledge of God and of the darkness that opposes God. This is a thread that runs through the whole discussion of the hiddenness of God. Anyone who has received even a tiny glimpse of the majesty, holiness, and righteousness of God will have an increased sense of the darkness, disorder, and malevolence that's loose in the world. These forces would swallow us up had not God set in motion his great plan to reclaim his creation. This is what Isaiah celebrates above all.

The verse "Truly, thou art a God who hidest thyself" is curiously placed because it comes in the midst of a passage of ecstatic praise. In fact, almost all of Isaiah 40–55 is ecstatic. It's the longest, most sustained hymn of praise to the power and purposes of God in the whole Bible. Yet the conditions in which those chapters were written were hopeless by any ordinary standards. The people of God had been dragged off to Babylon, where the colossal Mesopotamian gods dominated everything. They were forced to ponder the fact that their God had apparently abandoned them, along with his promises to them. When we remember that, it makes Isaiah's prophetic work seem truly miraculous. He writes that God is not dependent upon circumstances. God creates his own circumstances. God is not located simply within Israel. His power and promises encompass the entire created order.

It was widely noted, and noted with skepticism and even disdain by some, that every one of the funerals for the children of Sandy Hook school was held at a church. This does not answer the question of why God did not stop the shooter, that inexplicably damaged and lost young man, when he opened fire at the school. We do not know why God appeared to be absent. What we do know is that God was present in this way: he was present in the coming together of those who grieved with the families, to bring small lights into the blackness of their grief. They were not alone. There was something or Someone that drew the bereaved families deeper into the midst of the communities that continue to trust God even when he has hidden himself. Incomprehensible as it may seem, God is alive in the faith of his people wherever they are and in whatever condition.

The fact that God hides himself in the midst of revealing himself is paradoxically a testimony to his reality. Presence-in-absence is the theme of his self-disclosure. God isn't hidden because we are too stupid to find him, or too lazy, or not "spiritual" enough. He hides himself for his own reasons, and he reveals himself for his own reasons. If that were not so, God would not be God; God would be nothing more than a projection of our own religious ideas and wishes.

The Lord *hides* himself from us because he is God, and God *reveals* himself to us because *God is love* (1 John 4:8). That may not make sense, but sometimes Christians must be content with theological paradox. To know God in his Son Jesus Christ is to know that he is unconditionally Love unto the last drop of

God's own blood. In the cross and resurrection of his Son, God has given us everything that we need to live with alongside the terrors of his seeming absence.

Many churches do not use the phrase "he descended into hell" in the Apostles' Creed, but for many who have pondered its meaning, it is a central affirmation. In his death on the cross, Jesus descended into the hell of the absence of God. That's what the cry of dereliction on the cross means. "My God, my God, why have you forsaken me?" He experienced the absence of God his Father as no one else ever has, not even in the greatest extremity, because he experienced it for all of us. The Son of God underwent the opposite course: he came out from the light and went into the darkness . . . to be himself the light in our darkness.

The silence of God descended upon the cross on Good Friday.

And on the morning of the third day the sun rose upon the empty tomb.

PRAYER

Lord, we pray thee that thy grace may always precede and follow us, and make us continually to be given to all good works; through Jesus Christ our Lord, who liveth and reigneth with thee and the Holy Spirit, one God, now and for ever. Amen.

Daniel 3

"Our God whom we serve is able to deliver us from the burning fiery furnace; and he will deliver us out of your hand, O king. But if not, be it known to you, O king, that we will not serve your gods or worship the golden image which you have set up."

—DANIEL 3:17-18

Sometimes it seems that we should be asking whether the whole Christian community in America hasn't fallen prey to the gospel of prosperity, the gospel of success, the gospel of happiness in this world, the gospel of answered prayer. Sometimes I wonder if American culture might not be even more seductive than King Nebuchadnezzar's realm. After all, it was clear to the young Hebrews that Babylon really was pagan. YHWH of Israel, called the Most High God in the book of Daniel, was not worshiped in Babylon; his name was not known. In our country today, however, there is still a perceptible overlay of religion. Sometimes it's hard to find the boundary between the authentic worship of the God who is really God and something else that masquerades under that same name.

When King Nebuchadnezzar erected an image of gold on the plain of Dura, in the province of Babylon, however, there could have been no doubt in the minds of Shadrach, Meshach, and Abednego about whether it was really the Most High God wrapped in a Babylonian flag. It wasn't. It was an *idol*, pure and simple. Even so, there was a fairly potent threat attached to it.

If they didn't bow down to it and worship it, they were going to be thrown into a fiery furnace on the instant.

So what supernatural power gripped those young men? How did they find the courage to do what they did?

Let's direct our attention to an often overlooked but crucial part of the story. Read again verses 13 through 18 of Daniel 3 and notice the singular statement of Shadrach, Meshach, and Abednego as they confront the king: "Our God *is able* to deliver us and our God *will* deliver us; but *even if he does not* deliver us, we will not bow down to any other god."

This is a statement of ultimate trust in God *for his own sake*, a statement so radical as to make other statements about God look conditional, self-serving, and half-baked in comparison. This is not the familiar evangelistic technique of winning souls by recounting one tale after another of prayer requests answered. God is God, whether he chooses to intervene on the human stage in a particular way or not. His majesty, his righteousness, his worthiness to be worshiped do not depend on any given set of conditions that human beings might devise. The three young men believed that it was infinitely better to die praising the living God than it was to compromise his honor by acting as though he were no better than Nebuchadnezzar's image—a god bound to and limited by the needs and demands of his followers, a god who would be at the beck and call of those who claimed to worship him.

Well, you know the rest of the story. Nebuchadnezzar's storm troopers stoked up the furnace and forthwith threw the three young men into it, bound hand and foot. The flames of the furnace were so hot that they jumped out of the oven door and burned up the executioners. Nebuchadnezzar, sitting nearby in order to watch the grisly scene, jumped up in astonishment:

> "I see four men loose, walking in the midst of the fire, and they are not hurt; and the appearance of the fourth is like a son of the gods." (3:25)

Shadrach, Meshach, and Abednego stepped out of the furnace with not a hair on their heads or a thread of their garments so much as singed. And Nebuchadnezzar made a decree that no one was to speak anything against the God of Shadrach, Meshach, and Abednego, for "there is no other God who is able to deliver in this way" (3:28–29).

What we need now to remember about this magnificent story is that it was part of a literature written for the encouragement of the faithful who were undergoing fierce persecution. Throughout the centuries, this story has found its home in communities of believers who were probably not going to be delivered in this world. The book of Daniel is part of the literature of martyrdom.

God is supremely able, and worthy of worship for his own sake. Deliverance in this world is a sign of his greatness and "his mercy toward them that fear him," but it is not an end in itself. In those little words, "But if not," a whole history of pain, suffering, ambiguity, and seemingly unanswered prayer is summed up. In those little words, "Even if not," the determination of the Christian community to hold fast to the name of the Lord in spite of everything finds its noblest expression.

You will meet turnings in the road every day, turnings that, if taken, will lead you further and further away from the living God, deeper and deeper into the worship of the gods of the image-makers. As you come to these turnings in the way, perhaps you will think from time to time of Shadrach, Meshach, and Abednego, and how they said, "Our God is able to deliver us ... but if not, be it known to you, O King, that we will not serve the image which you have set up." For, you see, ultimately the story of the three young men in the fiery furnace, for all its thrilling qualities, is a story not of glory but of the cross. The story of Shadrach, Meshach, and Abednego has maintained its power over the centuries as a story cherished by those who would walk into the flames and would not come out again on this side—martyrs, slaves, prisoners, those who bore their witness in the midst of the world that hates God.

The worship of the living God may not bring us prosperity, may not bring us success, may not bring us advancement in this world, but he alone is worthy of worship for his own sake, he alone keeps his promises in the way that is best for us, he alone can and will vindicate the cause of his people. And for those who believe this, no road is too long, no fire too hot, no night too dark, no sacrifice too great, for truly, as King Nebuchadnezzar was forced to admit, "There is no other God who is able to deliver in this way."

May the Lord God of Hosts defend you for all your days and fill your hearts with the peace that passes human understanding.

PRAYER

Almighty and everlasting God, who in Christ hast revealed thy glory among the nations: Preserve the works of thy mercy, that thy Church throughout the world may persevere with steadfast faith in the confession of thy Name; through the same Jesus Christ our Lord, who liveth and reigneth with thee and the Holy Spirit, one God, for ever and ever. *Amen.*

Revelation 7:9–17

"For the Lamb in the midst of the throne will be their shepherd,
   and he will guide them to springs of living water;
   and God will wipe away every tear from their eyes."

—REVELATION 7:17

I have some big questions today: What is our ultimate standing? Who are we? Is there any permanent place for us in the universe, or is it as Macbeth feared?

And all our yesterdays have lighted fools
The way to dusty death. Out, out, brief candle!
Life's but a walking shadow, a poor player,
That struts and frets his hour upon the stage,
And then is heard no more. It is a tale
Told by an idiot, full of sound and fury,
Signifying nothing.[51]

It is very important for Christian people to think long and hard about the possibility that Macbeth might be right.

I am quite certain that all of us, whoever and wherever we are, want to know the answers to these ultimate questions: Is "dusty death" all there is? Does our tale signify anything? Are we going to be separated forever from those whose love has meant the whole world to us? One of the main reasons that Ecclesiastes is in the Bible is that we need to meditate very deeply on the fact that human nature in and of itself does not suggest positive answers to these questions.

> For the fate of the sons of men and the fate of beasts is the same; as one dies, so dies the other.... Man has no advantage over the beasts; for all is vanity. All go to one place; all are from the dust, and all turn to dust again. (Eccles. 3:19–20)

Every Christian should read Ecclesiastes from beginning to end at least once a year. It is the ultimate in pessimism. It gives us the lowdown on the human condition. It makes sentimental happy endings impossible.

Now, from this perspective, which I have deliberately drawn as gloomily as possible, let us look again at the reading from the book of Revelation:

> "These are they who have come out of the great tribulation; they have washed their robes and made them white in the blood of the Lamb.
>   Therefore are they before the throne of God,
>   and serve him day and night within his temple....
>   They shall hunger no more, neither thirst any more....
>   For the Lamb in the midst of the throne will be their
>   shepherd,
>   and he will guide them to springs of living water;
>   and God will wipe away every tear from their eyes."
>   (Rev. 7:14–17)

I hope that strikes you as powerfully on second reading as it does me. When we hear these verses read ceremonially at a funeral, or even in a Sunday morning service, they may very well go in one ear and straight out the other. The true force of these promises can only be felt when we have truly considered the alternatives.

What lies behind these great words from Revelation?

How are we to know that they are not just wishful thinking? Hasn't humanity developed past the point of relying on these fantasies? Isn't it really more courageous, more realistic, more evolved to acknowledge that heaven is nothing more than a projection of human longing? Isn't Ecclesiastes, in fact, a more honest book than Revelation?

It all depends on where Revelation came from. If this vision of the eternal life of God's people arose out of a mere human religious sensibility, then it is worth no more than the picture of a sunrise on an inspirational greeting card. But if, on the other hand, these words are actually promises from the living God, then that is a different matter.

The book of Revelation has taken a bad rap. It is by no means as weird as we have been led to believe. It is full of encouragement, hope, and comfort, especially for oppressed people. When Archbishop Desmond Tutu of South Africa was fighting the good fight against apartheid all those decades, he used to say, "Don't give up! Don't get discouraged! I've read the end of the book! We win!" The celestial vision arises out of the revelation of Jesus Christ himself, the Son of God who reigns in heaven and who has drawn back the curtain just for a moment to allow us a glimpse of God's future.

There comes a point in all our lives, I think, when we realize that the happier days are behind us; they are not going to come again; we are going to have to struggle; we are going to live with disappointment. That is the message of Ecclesiastes. Life is like this, and no amount of wishful thinking will make it different. The only power that can make it different is the power of God himself. That is what Revelation is about. It is about the power of God to create a completely new future:

> Then I saw a new heaven and a new earth; for the first heaven and the first earth had passed away.... And I saw the holy city, new Jerusalem, coming down out of heaven from God ... and I heard a loud voice from the throne saying, "Behold,

the dwelling of God is with humanity.... They shall be his people, and God himself will be with them; he will wipe away every tear from their eyes, and death shall be no more, neither shall there be mourning nor crying nor pain any more, for the former things have passed away." And he who sat upon the throne said, "Behold, I make all things new." (21:1–5)

In this world, we have to live in the tension between the resplendent assurance of Revelation and the tough-minded skepticism of Ecclesiastes. That tension between the two will not go away in this life.

I do not think anyone can ask any more searching questions about the visions of the Bible than I have asked myself. I have not put my trust in God's coming kingdom because I have avoided the tough issues of life. Bishop Tutu does not believe in God's radiant future because of an infantile need to believe in happy endings. He believes it, I believe it, you may believe it because the God who raised his Son Jesus Christ from the dead is a God who is able to keep his promises.

PRAYER

Almighty and everlasting God, give unto us the increase of faith, hope, and charity; and, that we may obtain that which thou dost promise, make us to love that which thou dost command; through Jesus Christ our Lord, who liveth and reigneth with thee and the Holy Spirit, one God, for ever and ever. Amen.

Romans 12

> *I appeal to you therefore, brothers and sisters, by the mercies of God,*
> *to present your bodies as a living sacrifice, holy and acceptable to God,*
> *which is your spiritual worship.*
>
> —ROMANS 12:1

Our reading from Romans, chapter 12, comes right after chapter 11. You may say "duh" to that, but what's important for us is not the sequence of numbers but the sequence of thought. Verse 1 of chapter 12, as you can see, begins with these words: "I appeal to you *therefore* ..." The word "therefore" holds the clue to everything that follows.

Romans 12 is a description of the saints. That is to say, it is a description of us. We are the saints. The church is made up of the saints, not individual exceptional "saintly" people, but a collective body of flawed and sinful people *to whom something has happened.* When we read and remember this text, we remember those things that have happened *to* us, and *for* us. That's the "therefore" that makes all the difference. That's what makes chapter 12 a reality. God's plan, outlined in chapters 1–11, is to expand the reach of his salvation through Jesus Christ beyond any conventionally religious boundaries that we can draw. Because this is so, we need always to be mindful of our special role in his plan, to be the image of Christ for those who do not yet know him. Chapter 12 is all about that special role.

With all due respect to a favorite hymn, there is a problem with "I sing a song of the saints of God." It lists various people whom we meet in church, in school, in lanes, in shops, in trains, or at tea (it's a very English hymn!) before the refrain:

They were all of them saints of God,
And I mean, God helping, to be one too.

What's wrong with that? Well, all the emphasis is on the "I," as in "I mean to be one too." Now, admittedly, there is that phrase "God helping," but it sounds decidedly secondary. The acting subject of the sentence is the "I." It sounds as if saint-hood is a future condition that I, *we, you* can attain someday if we just try hard enough. But this is not at all what our Scriptures tell us. It is the purpose of God that is primary, not what we have made up our minds to do. Saints are made in spite of themselves, by the action of the Holy Spirit. That is what has happened to us.

We don't "walk in newness of life" (Rom. 6:4) because we "mean to," or intend to. We are not raised from the dead because we mean to be, or intend to be. We are not embraced by the Father's glory because we mean to be or intend to be. We are raised from death into the eternal life of God because *God* means it, *God* intends it, *God* does it. You might not have noticed it, but God is the subject of most of the sentences in the Bible. God is the chief actor, and what God begins, God brings to completion. That is one of the most important themes of Romans, and indeed of Scripture as a whole.

When Paul is describing the saints, it is more like a description than an exhortation; the time-honored way of describing Paul's message is, "Become what you already are!" By the power of the Holy Spirit in the church, God *creates* a different kind of person, a person who fits the description in verses 9–21.

Paul describes the human predicament in Romans 7:

I do not understand my own actions. For I do not do what I want, but I do the very thing I hate.... So then it is no longer I that do it, but [the power of] sin which dwells within me. (vv. 15–17)

Surely we can all recognize this. It is a description of the struggle of the godly against their own worst impulses. But we are not left to our own resources in this predicament. Something has changed. The entire Christian message is grounded in the biblical announcement that God has done a new thing and will continue to do a new thing. The church is continually being conformed to the mind of Christ. Look again at our text:

I appeal to you therefore, brothers and sisters, by the mercies of God, to present your bodies as a living sacrifice, holy and acceptable to God, which is your spiritual worship. Do not be conformed to this world but be transformed by the renewal of your mind, so that you may prove what is the will of God.

Now, if you read this passage without the "therefore," you would think that the transformation Paul is speaking about is all up to us, that this is something that we manage by means of our own can-do attitude ("I mean to be one too"). On the contrary, there is a sense in which this transformation comes into being among us without our even realizing it. When you see this happen, you can't fail to recognize it, but often the transformed person does not know where the new power came from.

If you listen carefully to this passage in the context of Paul's whole letter, you'll see that it's the work of God from beginning to end—as the older prayer book says, "all our works [are] begun, continued and ended in thee." It is the work of God that the just requirement of the law is to be fulfilled in us. The message of Romans is about the power of God to bring his purposes to pass in spite of the obstacles we put in his way.

None of us can possibly be satisfied with the world as it is. We want to have things set to rights, and we want to be part of that movement. We would like to help. The promise of God is that this is exactly what God intends to do with us. Chapter 12 is a description of God's alternative mode of power. He can be trusted, not because we need something to believe in (though of course we do need that), *but because he is God*. God is the one who calls Christians of every age and station to walk in newness of life. That is not possible for us, but as our Lord himself said:

> "With men it is impossible, but not with God; for all things are possible with God." (Mark 10:27; Matt. 19:26)

It is even possible for sinners like you and me to be saints, not tomorrow, but today—because it is God's doing.

PRAYER

Almighty and merciful God, of whose only gift it cometh that thy faithful people do unto thee true and laudable service: Grant, we beseech thee, that we may run without stumbling to obtain thy heavenly promises; through Jesus Christ our Lord, who liveth and reigneth with thee and the Holy Spirit, one God, now and for ever. *Amen.*

1 Peter 4:12–19; 1 Thessalonians 5:1–11

For the time has come for judgment to begin with the household of God.

—1 PETER 4:17

As a good many commentators have noted, the Advent season actually begins *before* the first Sunday of Advent. It's a seven-week season, beginning after All Saints' Day. The lectionary begins to take on a note of foreboding. Advent begins in the dark. Saint Paul writes, "As to the times and the seasons, brothers and sisters, ... the day of the Lord will come like a thief in the night. When people say, 'There is peace and security,' then sudden destruction will come upon them ... and there will be no escape" (1 Thess. 5:1–3).

The intended effect of the readings at this time of year is to disturb our peace and security. The purpose of this seven-week season is to take an unflinching inventory of darkness. Advent is a time to focus on sin and judgment, despite the deep resistance throughout the church to sitting with these themes.

How shall we preach judgment? If we are unable to live with the thought of the judgment of God because we don't want to allow it into our tidy concept of God as loving, forgiving, and accepting, then what we need to do is envision Afghan girls I read about in the *Globe and Mail* one time who were blinded and disfigured by an attack of acid sprayed in their faces because they had the temerity to go to school. If we are reluctant to think about judgment, we need to call to mind the Spanish *desaparecidos*, the people who wrote editorials or joined political groups in opposition to Franco, who were taken from their families under cover of darkness and never seen again. If we remember them, and any number of other victims, then let us ask ourselves, do we want a world without the wrath of God? If we summon these examples, the words of God to the prophet Isaiah seem more suitable: I *was angry, I smote Israel, I hid my face and was angry.* In such circumstances, we can understand that the judgment of God upon all evil is good, right, and necessary. A culture of impunity is nothing less than hell.

The trouble is, as I am sure you have already figured out, that we don't mind God being wrathful against somebody other than us. The difficulty comes when judgment draws close to *us*, to *our* friends, to *our* group, to *our* favorite cause. How are we to understand the words of Peter? How shall the church stand first in line for the dreadful day of judgment?

We begin to do this by remembering that the church is not a collection of autonomous individuals but a family, brothers and sisters of Christ by adoption and grace, "fellow citizens with the saints and members of the household of God, built upon the foundation of the apostles and prophets, Christ Jesus himself being the cornerstone, in whom the whole structure is joined together and grows into a holy temple in the Lord" (Eph. 2:19–21). When we reflect upon *that* gospel truth, doesn't it become clear that there is nothing, not even God's own judgment, that can destroy a structure built upon the cornerstone that is God's only begotten Son? In that sense, truly the fellowship of the baptized has already passed through the judgment, as John says (John 5:24). In that sense the words of Paul in our reading from 1 Thessalonians are also true: "God has not destined us for wrath, but to obtain salvation through our Lord Jesus Christ" (5:9). This is true security, a security that the empires of the world with all their might cannot pretend to convey.

But this true security does not simply lift us clear of this world. We must live this perilous existence along with everybody else. This is a world where cancer strikes the just and the unjust indiscriminately, where punishment is meted out to those who do *not* deserve it while those who *do* deserve it go free, where the poor get poorer and the rich get richer. This is the world of Advent, a world that makes no moral sense to the unaided eye. Advent begins in the dark. Anyone that tells you otherwise is living in denial.

"But you are not in darkness, brothers and sisters," continues the apostle Paul. "You are not in darkness for the day [of judgment] to surprise you like a thief. For you are all children of light and children of the day; we are not children of the night or of darkness. So then let us not sleep, as others do, but let us keep awake and be sober" (1 Thess. 5:4-6).

As children of the day, we stand first in line at the bar of judgment by repenting of our sins and the sins of the whole church and the sins of the whole world. We are involved in each other because God was first involved in us. The wrath of God and the love of God are two faces of the same thing. The world will be purged of its iniquity in the consuming fire of the second coming of the Lord Jesus Christ. That is the Advent theme. He will come again to set all things right. In the meantime we take up the weapons of his warfare: "Since we belong to the day, let us ... put on the breastplate of faith and love, and for a helmet the hope of salvation" (1 Thess. 5:8). Anything we can do—anything at all, however small or large—any deed of kindness or generosity or courage that eases the load of someone else or brings truth and justice to light—is a sign of the advent of the one who is and who was and who is to come, the Almighty (Rev. 1:8).

"The time has come for judgment to begin with the household of God," but "God has not destined us for wrath, but to obtain salvation through our Lord Jesus Christ, who died for us so that whether we wake or sleep we might live with him. Therefore encourage one another and build one another up,

just as you are doing" (I Thess. 5:9–11), and the power of the
Ruler of the universe will be your strength and your shield,
your rock and your fortress, your shepherd and your judge,
your Savior and Redeemer, your Lord and your God.

PRAYER

O God, whose blessed Son was manifested that he might destroy the works of the devil and make us children of God and
heirs of eternal life: Grant us, we beseech thee, that, having this
hope, we may purify ourselves even as he is pure; that, when he
shall appear again with power and great glory, we may be made
like unto him in his eternal and glorious kingdom; where with
thee, O Father, and thee, O Holy Ghost, he liveth and reigneth
ever, one God, world without end. *Amen.*

Mark 13

"Take heed; I have told you all things beforehand."

—MARK 13:23

I f you know your Christian calendar, you're getting goose bumps. Advent is close; the lectionary readings from Scripture start getting apocalyptic in November. The turn of the year is the church's way of looking backward and forward at the same time, and acknowledging the one who holds both the past and the future. "I am the Alpha and the Omega," says the Lord God, "the first and the last," the beginning and the end, "who is and who was and who is to come" (Rev. 1:8, 17).

The reading for this week, Mark 13, speaks of wars, earthquakes, eclipses, people running for their lives, demonic figures appearing in the murky light, cosmic cataclysm, and then the Son of God riding in on a cloud with an army of angels and archangels. It really is quite thrilling in some ways, but utterly alien and baffling in others, especially the parts about how there is going to be more suffering and more calamity than the world has ever known.

One part of Mark 13 that jumps out at me is that "in those days there will be such tribulation as has not been from the beginning of the creation until now, and never will be" (v. 19). Isn't this a rather morbid exaggeration, as if we are supposed to take some delight in hearing about it? It seems almost pathological. And yet the question that we all ask, if we are serious about faith and life, is, "Why are things so bad in the world? Why is there so much evil and suffering?"

One of the reasons that the Christian gospel makes sense is that it takes fully into account the sadness and brokenness and downright wickedness of this life. Suffering and distress are inescapable in a world fallen away from God. We have been warned: "Behold, I have told you all things beforehand" (Mark 13:23). Disease, loss, suffering, and death are inescapable in the Christian life. If we continue to speak only of peace and love when Jesus has predicted conflict and catastrophe, then we have simply refused to hear a substantial part of his message. There is a link between suffering and the kingdom of God—a close connection. That's what the readings about the end of the ages tell us.

"Tribulation" (*thlipsis* in Greek) is a word that the New Testament uses to describe the signs of the coming kingdom. It's not just ordinary suffering. *Thlipsis* is a revelatory word; it points beyond itself to the coming triumph of the Lord. "I have said these things to you," says Jesus Christ in the Gospel of John, "that in me you may have peace. In this world, you will have tribulation (*thlipsis*); but be of good cheer, I have overcome the world" (John 16:33). Jesus says these words an hour before he goes to be betrayed and given up for torture and execution.

The curious and paradoxical thing about the New Testament teachings concerning the last things is that they produce hope, not despair; confidence, not fear. Hope and *confidence*—those are the key ideas. Look, says Jesus as he stands with his little group of disciples overlooking the city of Jerusalem, the transition from this world to the coming reign of God will not happen without a fight to the death. That's why there's so much military imagery in both the Old Testament and the New Testament. The "ruler of this world," as Jesus calls Satan in John's Gospel, will not go down without a battle. He is a foe too powerful for unaided human beings; but, as in the story of the servant of the prophet Elisha in the book of Kings, there are unseen horses and chariots of fire guaranteeing the promise of God (2 Kings 6:17).

Advent does not mean that we can sit back and ignore the predicament of humanity because God is going to come in on a cloud and clean it all up. The nature of God's future is that it impinges on our lives right now. God's future exerts a pressure upon us. That's what the apocalyptic New Testament language of this season really means when it tells us that the time is short. In each life, in each action of a Christian believer, we act as if it were our last act. This is somewhat tricky to talk about because we don't mean that every moment has to be a crisis—that would be an intolerable way to live. Perhaps the best way to think about it is that the knowledge of the coming of the Lord gives a significance to each act of mercy that it would not otherwise have, and a confidence that God will fit it all into his great purpose.

Yes, there will be suffering. Yes, there will be horrible, inexplicable violence, and much of it will seem utterly without any redemptive meaning. But there is nothing that can happen that is not subject to the sovereignty of God. This was the faith that electrified the ancient world when people heard the preaching of the apostles and evangelists—many of whom would die violently at the hands of the occupying oppressors. No suffering can be properly understood until the Lord comes—but he will come. God is accomplishing his purposes in spite of all appearances to the contrary. Nothing can lie beyond the power of God to redeem and transform. We believe this because we have been seized by the unique authority of the voice of Jesus Christ.

When you know that our Redeemer has warned you that his kingdom will arise out of great suffering, then you will not be taken by surprise if your faith costs you something. What you will have, however, throughout it all, are *faith* and *hope*. If you know that God the Creator and Judge of all things is truly sovereign over all of human and cosmic history, then your small concerns will begin to become part of a great pattern, and they will worry you less as your commitment to your fellow Christians means more and more. If you know that the reconciliation of all things is the grand design of the Creator of the universe, then your own individual and communal acts of faithfulness to one another become signs in this world of the world to come. If you know that "the one who endures to the end will be saved" (Mark 13:13), then you will be given courage and strength to meet whatever happens. Even though the apocalyptic language of Advent is grand and cosmic, nevertheless it is in the daily round of small but self-forgetful actions of faithfulness that the future of God is made present.

PRAYER

Blessed Lord, who hast caused all holy Scriptures to be written for our learning: Grant that we may in such wise hear them, read, mark, learn, and inwardly digest them, that, by patience and comfort of thy holy Word, we may embrace and ever hold fast the blessed hope of everlasting life, which thou hast given us in our Savior Jesus Christ; who liveth and reigneth with thee and the Holy Spirit, one God, for ever and ever. *Amen.*

Matthew 25:31–46

"'Come, O blessed of my Father, inherit the kingdom prepared for you from the foundation of the world.'"

—MATTHEW 25:34

Today we read through the last days of Jesus's ministry from the Gospel of Matthew. As the curtain goes up for what seems to be the final act, the Lord is about to be betrayed. He will be arraigned, tried, and condemned as a blasphemer by the world's noblest religion and executed as an insurrectionist by the world's most powerful government. At the eleventh hour, we find him speaking privately to his disciples almost for the last time, and this is what he says: "When the Son of man comes in his glory, and all the angels with him, then he will sit on his glorious throne. Before him will be gathered all the nations, and he will separate them one from another as a shepherd separates the sheep from the goats" (Matt. 25:31–32).

On that last day when the Son of Man "comes again in glory to judge the quick and the dead," he will be surrounded with all the unmistakable accoutrements of majesty and dominion. He will sit on his throne of glory, and at his feet, spread out before him, will be all of human history in unimaginable completeness. Julius Caesar and Napoleon will be there; Genghis Khan and Joan of Arc will be there; Martin Luther and Catherine the Great and Voltaire and Stalin will be there. Don't be sidetracked by literal-minded speculations about where, when, or how this is going to happen. What we are intended to feel is not intellectual curiosity but the overwhelming majesty and solemnity of the event. The impression burned into our hearts today is this: on that climactic and final day, *we will be there.*

Jesus Christ will be the Judge, and no one else. To him "all hearts are open, all desires known, and from [him] no secrets are hid."[52] The Lord will put the chosen sheep at his right hand and say, "I was hungry and you gave me food, I was thirsty and you gave me drink, I was a stranger and you welcomed me, I was naked and you clothed me, I was sick and you visited me, I was in prison and you came to me." The response comes back, "Lord, when did we do all those things?" "And the King shall answer and say unto them, 'Verily I say unto you, Inasmuch as ye have done it unto one of the least of these my brethren, ye have done it unto me'" (vv. 35–40).

We have heard these famous lines many times. Today, can we recover something of their startling originality? In the time of Jesus, the Messiah was expected to be a kingly figure, so there was nothing surprising there. What was emphatically *not* expected was that he would actually be present in the lowliest of the low. We might have more logically expected the Judge to commend his disciples for heroic deeds, bold achievements, glorious sacrifices; instead, they are acknowledged and welcomed as those who have performed tiny, insignificant acts of charity toward people who appear to be of no account.

Notice the response of those on Jesus's right hand when they are told that they are about to inherit the kingdom. They are amazed. They did not know that they had ministered to the hidden Christ among the "least" of these his brethren. Notice also the response of those on the left hand. They are not aware either. Apparently they expected to be commended. It looks as though there are going to be surprises for everyone. He who congratulates himself on having done enough is precisely the one who has not. The person who trembles to think of herself before the judgment seat is closer to the kingdom of heaven than the one who complacently assumes she is on the side of the angels. We cannot rely on any known good deeds; the complete astonishment of the redeemed and the shattered confidence of the condemned are clear evidence of this.

The parable of the last judgment is not about totaling up one's own good deeds. It is about serving Christ the King. The teaching about the "least of these" should not be detached from the titanic figure of Christ as the final arbiter of the destiny of all creation. The division of the sheep and the goats is not based on who is good and who is bad. It is based on honoring Christ by serving him as he is present in the lives of those who are invisible to the world of power mongering. If Jesus Christ is not Lord, then there is nothing here but moralism, and the Gospel of Matthew does not teach moralism. Matthew teaches Christ the Lord, which is a very different thing. It is the living presence of Christ in the midst of the community that makes the difference.

The revolutionary aspect of this would not be as obvious to us if we had no letters from Paul the apostle. In 1 Corinthians, we read these ringing words: "As in Adam all die, even so in Christ shall all be made alive" (1 Cor. 15:22). Everything depends on being *in Christ*. If Christ is going to judge me by all the things I have not done to help my neighbor who is hungry, cold, sick, or in prison, then I am doomed indeed. I cannot stand before this tribunal. I know that. But I know also that *in Christ* things can happen in me that I cannot do alone.

Those who are in Christ, who are incorporated into him, are being remade day by day into people who will someday say, "When did we see thee, Lord?" in glad amazement because they did not even notice that they were ministering to him in the small actions of mercy that were performed. At the last judgment, "Adam" will disappear into outer darkness forever, and we will be refashioned in the image of him who is King of kings and Lord of lords among the least, the last, and the lost.[53]

This Master cares so much for the least, the last, and the lost that he is willing to die even for such poor specimens as you and me, covering our unrighteousness with his righteousness, offering his life to save us from death, victorious over the old Adam, the Judge judged in our place. He has compensated for our too-short list of good deeds by his one great deed. Now by his indwelling Spirit he will make us into those who will some-day hear the blessed words, "Come, O blessed of my Father, inherit the kingdom prepared for you from the foundation of the world."

PRAYER

Almighty and everlasting God, whose will it is to restore all things in thy well-beloved Son, the King of kings and Lord of lords: Mercifully grant that the peoples of the earth, divided and enslaved by sin, may be freed and brought together under his most gracious rule; who liveth and reigneth with thee and the Holy Spirit, one God, now and for ever. Amen.

NOTES

....

1. Northrop Frye, *The Great Code* (New York: Harcourt Brace Jova-novich, 1982), 213.

2. Annie Dillard, *Teaching a Stone to Talk* (New York: Harper & Row, 1988), 40.

3. Dorothy L. Sayers, "The Dogma Is the Drama," in *The Whimsical Christian: 18 Essays* (Collier Books, 1987).

4. "We Sing of God, the Mighty Source," 1982 Episcopal Hymnal, #387. The full text of four verses is breathtaking. Christopher Smart's hymn texts are among the best ever written and should be better known. Smart spent seven years in an "insane asylum," the horrific nature of which in the eighteenth century can only be imagined, but he was well known in London literary circles and is now recognized as a significant English poet.

5. Most of the biblical quotations in this book come from the Revised Standard Version, although some emanate from various translations, and some are hybrids of different translations that lent themselves to sermonic use.

6. George Herbert, "The Windows" (1633), https://www.poetryfoundation.org/poems/50695/the-windows-56d22df68ff95.

7. This is not to denigrate Lutherans, Moravians, and others who traditionally observe the liturgical year. My experience, however, tells me that Episcopalians have been particularly faithful in this regard even through manifold cultural changes.

8. Isaac Watts, "O God, Our Help in Ages Past."

9. From Thomas Cranmer's Prayer of Consecration, Book of Common Prayer.

10. Hymn, "Joy to the World."

11. 1979 Book of Common Prayer, 368.

12. Edwin Hoskyns, *The Fourth Gospel* (London: Faber & Faber, 1947), 186.

13. Reginald Fuller, *Interpreting the Miracles* (Norwich, UK: Fletcher & Son, 1963), 117.

14. This distinction was famously made by Dietrich Bonhoeffer in his book *The Cost of Discipleship.*

15. "The King of Love My Shepherd Is," by Henry Williams Baker (1821–1877), paraphrase of Psalm 23.

16. Alex Kuczynski, "Valentine's Day Times Three: The Horror!" *New York Times,* January 8, 1998.

17. Taylor Branch, *Pillar of Fire: America in the King Years, 1963–65* (New York: Simon & Schuster, 1998), 613 (emphasis added).

18. As Kenneth Slack says in his book about the Psalms, *New Light on Old Songs.*

19. *The Letters of J. R. R. Tolkien,* ed. Humphrey Carpenter (Boston: Houghton Mifflin, 2000; first published in Great Britain by George Allen & Unwin, 1981), 93 (emphasis added).

20. Aleksandr Solzhenitsyn, *The Gulag Archipelago,* pt. 4, chap. 1.

21. "Whatever Happened to Repentance?" *Christianity Today,* February 4, 2002.

22. Vincent Taylor, *The Gospel according to St. Mark* (London: Macmillan, 1952), 446.

23. Vincent Taylor's phrase, often repeated by others.

24. C. S. Lewis, *The Lion, the Witch, and the Wardrobe.*

25. Paul Ricoeur, *The Symbolism of Evil* (New York: Harper & Row, 1967), 63.

26. "Go to Dark Gethsemane," by James Montgomery (1771–1854), in 1982 Episcopal Hymnal, #171.

27. Stephen Mitchell, *Into the Whirlwind* (New York: Doubleday, 1979). This text was also published with an introduction as *The Book of Job* (San Francisco: North Point, 1987).

28. RSV and Stephen Mitchell translations.

29. John Calvin, *Sermons from Job* (Grand Rapids: Baker Book House, 1979), 123.

30. Israel Finkelstein and Neil A. Silberman, *The Bible Unearthed: Archaeology's New Vision of Ancient Israel and the Origin of Its Sacred Texts* (New York: Free Press, 2001). Review by Phyllis Trible, *New York Times Book Review,* February 4, 2001.

31. Phrase from the Episcopal Book of Common Prayer.

32. A phrase taken from Brendan Gill's review of *Who's Afraid of Virginia Woolf?* entitled "In Vino Veritas," *New Yorker,* April 12, 1976.

33. *Hamlet,* act 2, scene 2.

34. Artur Weise, *The Psalms: A Commentary* (Philadelphia: Westminster, 1962), 774.

35. Samuel Terrien, *The Psalms and Their Meaning for Today* (Indianapolis: Bobbs-Merrill, 1952), 170.

36. Gerhard von Rad, *Genesis* (Philadelphia: Westminster, 1972), 239.

37. J. Louis Martyn, "From Paul to Flannery O'Connor with the Power of Grace," *Katallagete* 7, no. 4 (1981) (emphasis added).

38. Eucharistic Prayer B, The Book of Common Prayer, 368.

39. The Collect for Purity, Holy Eucharist I, Book of Common Prayer.

40. Gerhard von Rad, *Genesis* (Philadelphia: Westminster, 1972), 80–81.

41. Karl Barth, *Church Dogmatics* III/4 (Edinburgh: T&T Clark, 1956), 450.

42. Annie Dillard, *Teaching a Stone to Talk* (New York: Harper & Row, 1988), 40.

43. Quoted in Timothy Garton Ash, "The Truth about Dictatorship," *New York Review of Books*, February 19, 1998, 36–37.

44. C. S. Lewis, *Mere Christianity* (New York: Macmillan, 1953), 59.

45. Translation of 5:21 by Ernst Käsemann in his commentary on Romans (Grand Rapids: Eerdmans, 1980). He also uses "sin gained dominion" to translate 5:17.

46. "Lead On, O King Eternal," by Ernest W. Shurtleff (1887).

47. Lewis, *Mere Christianity*, 161.

48. Book of Common Prayer, Eucharistic Rite I.

49. Matthew calls it the kingdom of heaven.

50. Act 4, scene 3, line 83.

51. *Macbeth*, act 5, scene 5.

52. Collect for Purity, Book of Common Prayer, Holy Eucharist, Rites I and II.

53. "The least, the last, and the lost" is a phrase of Robert Farrar Capon.